THE
CHOCOLATE
COOKBOOK

THE
CHOCOLATE
COOKBOOK

LUXURIOUS TREATS FOR TOTAL INDULGENCE: 135 IRRESISTIBLE
RECIPES SHOWN IN 260 STUNNING PHOTOGRAPHS

Christine McFadden
Christine France

LORENZ BOOKS

This edition is published by Lorenz Books, an imprint of
Anness Publishing Ltd,
Hermes House,
88–89 Blackfriars Road,
London SE1 8HA
tel. 020 7401 2077; fax 020 7633 9499

www.lorenzbooks.com; www.annesspublishing.com

If you like the images in this book and would like to
investigate using them for publishing, promotions or
advertising, please visit our website
www.practicalpictures.com for more information.

UK agent: The Manning Partnership Ltd;
    tel. 01225 478444; fax 01225 478440;
    sales@manning-partnership.co.uk
UK distributor: Grantham Book Services Ltd;
    tel. 01476 541080; fax 01476 541061;
    orders@gbs.tbs-ltd.co.uk
North American agent/distributor: National Book
    Network; tel. 301 459 3366; fax 301 429 5746;
    www.nbnbooks.com
Australian agent/distributor: Pan Macmillan Australia;
    tel. 1300 135 113; fax 1300 135 103;
    customer.service@macmillan.com.au
New Zealand agent/distributor: David Bateman Ltd;
    tel. (09) 415 7664; fax (09) 415 8892

Publisher: Joanna Lorenz
Project Editor: Amy Christian
Recipes: Catherine Atkinson, Jane Bamforth, Alex Barker,
Valerie Barrett, Judy Bastyra, Jacqueline Clark, Carole
Clements, Joanna Farrow, Brian Glover, Nicola Graimes,
Juliet Harbutt, Christine Ingram, Becky Johnson, Lucy
Knox, Marlene Spieler, Kate Whiteman, Rosemary
Wilkinson, Elizabeth Wolf-Cohen, Jenni Wright
Photography: Karl Adamson, Edward Allwright, Steve
Baxter, Nicki Dowey, James Duncan, Michelle Garrett,
Amanda Heywood, Janine Hosegood, David King, Don
Last, William Adams-Lingwood, Thomas Odulate, Craig
Robertson, Bridget Sargeson, Sam Stowell
Production Controller: Claire Rae

Picture Acknowledgements
Thanks to the following picture libraries for supplying
additional images in the book. Bridgeman Art Library:
pp198, 199 (tl), 199, 200(bl), 202 (tr), 210 (t), 215 (b),
216 (t), 217 (t). Corbis: pp204, 205, 206 (tr).
    Other pictures supplied courtesy of Nestlé Rowntree
Ltd: pp 206 (tl), 207 (bl). The Nestlé name and image is
reproduced with the kind permission of Société des
Produits Nestlé S.A.

ETHICAL TRADING POLICY
At Anness Publishing we believe that business should
be conducted in an ethical and ecologically sustainable
way, with respect for the environment and a proper
regard to the replacement of the natural resources
we employ.
    As a publisher, we use a lot of wood pulp to make
high-quality paper for printing, and that wood
commonly comes from spruce trees. We are therefore
currently growing more than 750,000 trees in three
Scottish forest plantations: Berrymoss (130 hectares/
320 acres), West Touxhill (125hectares/305 acres) and
Deveron Forest (75 hectares/185 acres). The forests
we manage contain more than 3.5 times the number of
trees employed each year in making paper for the books
we manufacture.
    Because of this ongoing ecological investment
programme, you, as our customer, can have the pleasure
and reassurance of knowing that a tree is being
cultivated on your behalf to naturally replace the
materials used to make the book you are holding.
    Our forestry programme is run in accordance with the
UK Woodland Assurance Scheme (UKWAS) and will be
certified by the internationally recognized
Forest Stewardship Council (FSC). The FSC is a non-
government organization dedicated to promoting
responsible management of the world's forests.
Certification ensures forests are managed in an
environmentally sustainable and socially responsible
way. For further information about this scheme, go
to www.annesspublishing.com/trees.

A CIP catalogue record for this book is available from
the British Library.

Recipes in this book previously appeared in
The Chocolate Bible

PUBLISHER'S NOTE
Although the advice and information in this book are
believed to be accurate and true at the time of going to
press, neither the authors nor the publisher can accept
any legal responsibility or liability for any errors or
omissions that may be made.

NOTES
For all recipes, quantities are given in both
metric and imperial measures and, where
appropriate, in standard cups and spoons. Follow
one set of measures, but not a mixture, because
they are not interchangeable.
    Standard spoon and cup measures are level.
1 tsp = 5ml, 1 tbsp = 15ml, 1 cup = 250ml/8fl oz.
Australian standard tablespoons are 20ml.
Australian readers should use 3 tsp in place of
1 tbsp for measuring small quantities.
    American pints are 16fl oz/2 cups. American
readers should use 20fl oz/2.5 cups in place of
1 pint when measuring liquids.
    Electric oven temperatures in this book are for
conventional ovens. When using a fan oven, the
temperature will probably need to be reduced
by about 10–20°C/20–40°F. Since ovens vary,
you should check with your manufacturer's
instruction book for guidance.
    The nutritional analysis given for each recipe is
calculated per portion (i.e. serving or item),
unless otherwise stated. If the recipe gives a
range, such as Serves 4–6, then the nutritional
analysis will be for the smaller portion size,
i.e. 6 servings. Measurements for sodium do not
include salt added to taste.
    Medium (US large) eggs are used unless
otherwise stated.
    Front cover shows Chocolate Redcurrant Torte,
for recipe see page 50.

Contents

Introduction

One of the greatest treasures ever discovered was the bean from the Theobroma cacao *tree, the original source of chocolate. Smooth in texture, intense in taste, subtly perfumed and elegant to behold, chocolate is a rich source of sensory pleasure, adored by almost everyone.*

COOKING WITH CHOCOLATE

This book will introduce you to recipes for many new and unusual chocolate creations, as well as covering all the traditional favourites. With over 135 recipes, you will find mouthwatering ideas for every kind of chocolate cake imaginable, from the comforting Chocolate Chip Walnut Loaf to the decadent White Chocolate Cappuccino Cake. With over 260 colour photographs accompanying the recipes, perfect results are guaranteed every time.

A chapter on hot desserts will devastate you with Hot Chocolate Zabaglione, Hot Mocha Rum Soufflés

and Chocolate Pecan Pie. Recipes for chocolate tarts and chilled desserts include classics such as luscious Mississippi Mud Pie and Tiramisù; and there are plenty of recipes for cookies and little cakes. You will also see how to make your own chocolates and truffles, which make lovely gifts to delight family and friends, and the most deeply indulgent chocolate drinks, perfect for those cold winter nights.

The beautifully illustrated recipes conclude with an informative section on chocolate sauces and toppings, containing ideas and inspiration for exciting ways to finish off your cakes

and desserts. There are also tips on melting, tempering and making perfect decorations, such as curls, squiggles, and even chocolate leaves.

DRINK OF THE GODS

This book is a celebration of a divine food, and divine it really is – translated from the Greek, *theobroma* literally means "food of the gods".

As well as an inspiring recipe collection, the book explores the fascinating history of chocolate. In the final chapter, The Guide to

BELOW: *The classic American Mississippi Mud Pie with its fluffy chocolate filling.*

ABOVE: *Magic Chocolate Mud Pudding is delicious with yogurt or ice cream.*

ABOVE: *Rich and tasty Black Forest Gateau is always a favourite.*

ABOVE: *Sweet and irresistible Chocolate Crackle-tops make the perfect snack.*

Chocolate, the story of chocolate is traced from its use by the Maya in Central America to Spain and the rest of Europe, and then back across the Atlantic to the United States. It becomes clear that since the earliest days of its discovery, chocolate has woven intricate links among people on every level – national, cultural, social, economic and spiritual. Chocolate has never failed to make an impact, provoking comment from the church, the medical profession, scientists, social reformers and royalty. Over the centuries it has been eagerly consumed in one form or another by all levels of society.

In a section on cultivation and processing, learn where and how cacao is grown and harvested, and how it is fermented and dried. The book then goes on to trace the transformation of cacao from bean to beverage and from beverage to confectionery, and describes how this was made possible on a commercial scale.

The international world of chocolate, including the very different characteristics of each country's chocolate, is also investigated. Flavourings and sweetness may vary, but what unites them is that smooth, sensuous, melt-in-the-mouth quality that is so hard to resist.

Finally, the book delves into the physiology and psychology of chocolate, covering nutrition, craving and addiction, passion and pleasure. The taste and quality of chocolate is also examined, as we look at the specialist world of quality chocolate and fillings, demystifying terms such as cacao solids, praline and ganache.

The book is not only a celebration of a wonderful food, it will also fascinate and instruct you in the history and production of this unique gastronomic treasure. Indulge yourself in a visual chocolate feast and accept the fact that if chocolate is not already an intrinsic part of your life, this book will make sure that it becomes so.

Small bakes and cakes

There's no end to the ways you can use chocolate in small cakes and cookies. Start the day with a warm Brioche au Chocolat, or treat yourself at coffee time to rich Nut and Chocolate Chip Brownies. Or, if you're after something special, Chocolate Cinnamon Tuiles are the perfect choice.

Mocha Viennese swirls

Some temptations just can't be resisted. Put out a plate of these melt-in-the-mouth marvels and watch them vanish. If the mixture is too stiff to pipe, soften it with a little more black coffee.

MAKES ABOUT 20

115g/4oz plain (semisweet) chocolate, broken into squares

200g/7oz/scant 1 cup unsalted (sweet) butter, softened

50g/2oz/6 tbsp icing (confectioners') sugar

30ml/2 tbsp strong black coffee

200g/7oz/1¾ cups plain (all-purpose) flour

50g/2oz/½ cup cornflour (cornstarch)

TO DECORATE

about 20 blanched almonds

150g/5oz plain (semisweet) chocolate

1 Preheat the oven to 190°C/375°F/Gas 5. Grease two baking sheets. Melt the chocolate in a bowl over a pan of hot water. Cream the butter and icing sugar in a bowl until smooth and pale. Beat in the melted chocolate, then the strong black coffee.

2 Sift the flour and cornflour over the mixture. Fold in lightly and evenly to make a soft mixture.

3 Spoon the mixture into a piping bag fitted with a large star nozzle and pipe about 20 swirls on the baking sheets, allowing room for spreading during baking.

4 Press an almond into the centre of each swirl. Bake for about 15 minutes or until the biscuits are firm and just beginning to brown.

5 Leave the swirls to cool for about 10 minutes on the baking sheets, then, with a spatula, lift carefully on to a wire rack to cool completely.

6 When the biscuits are cool, melt the chocolate in a bowl over a pan of hot water. Remove the bowl from the pan and dip the base of each swirl into the chocolate until coated. Place on a sheet of baking parchment and leave to set.

Nutritional information: Energy 210kcal/877kJ; Protein 2.2g; Carbohydrate 21.3g, of which sugars 11.2g; Fat 13.5g, of which saturates 7.6g; Cholesterol 22mg; Calcium 28mg; Fibre 0.8g; Sodium 64mg.

Chocolate marzipan cookies

These delicious crisp little cookies have an almond surprise inside and are the perfect choice for anyone with a sweet tooth. If the dough is too sticky to roll, chill it for 30 minutes then try again.

MAKES ABOUT 36

200g/7oz/scant 1 cup unsalted (sweet) butter, softened
200g/7oz/generous 1 cup light muscovado (brown) sugar
1 egg
300g/11oz/2¾ cups plain (all-purpose) flour
60ml/4 tbsp unsweetened cocoa powder
200g/7oz white almond paste
115g/4oz white chocolate, broken into squares

1 Preheat the oven to 190°C/375°F/ Gas 5. Lightly grease two baking sheets. Cream the butter with the sugar in a large bowl until pale and fluffy. Add the egg and beat well.

2 Sift the flour and cocoa over the mixture. Stir in, first with a wooden spoon, then with clean hands, pressing the mixture together to make a fairly soft dough.

3 Roll out about half the dough on a lightly floured surface to a thickness of about 5mm/¼in. Using a 5cm/2in round cutter, cut out circles, re-rolling the dough as required until you have 36 circles.

4 Cut the almond paste into 36 equal pieces. Roll into balls, flatten and place one on each round of dough. Roll out the remaining dough, cut out more rounds, then place on top of the almond paste. Press the dough edges to seal.

5 Bake for 10 minutes, or until they are well risen and the surfaces are beginning to crack. Cool on the baking sheet for about 2 minutes, then finish cooling on a wire rack.

6 Melt the white chocolate, then drizzle it over the cookies, or spoon into a paper piping bag and pipe a design on to the cookies.

Nutritional information: Energy 137kcal/576kJ; Protein 1.9g; Carbohydrate 18.1g, of which sugars 11.6g; Fat 6.9g, of which saturates 3.8g; Cholesterol 17mg; Calcium 31mg; Fibre 0.6g; Sodium 57mg.

Chocolate macaroons

Perfect for tea-time, chocolate macaroons are a great alternative to ordinary macaroons – the almond flavour is wonderfully enhanced by the addition of the chocolate.

MAKES 24

50g/2oz plain (semisweet) chocolate, chopped into small pieces
115g/4oz/1 cup blanched almonds
225g/8oz/1 cup sugar
2 egg whites
2.5ml/¹/₂ tsp vanilla extract
1.5ml/¹/₄ tsp almond extract
icing (confectioners') sugar, for dusting

1 Preheat the oven to 150°C/300°F/Gas 2. Line two large baking sheets with baking parchment. Melt the chocolate in the top of a double boiler, or in a heatproof bowl set over a pan of simmering water.

2 Grind the almonds finely in a food processor, blender or nut grinder. Transfer to a mixing bowl. Add the sugar, egg whites, vanilla extract and almond extract and stir to blend. Stir the melted chocolate into the mixture. The mixture should just hold its shape. If it is too soft, chill it in the refrigerator for 15 minutes.

3 Use a teaspoon and your hands to shape the dough into walnut-size balls. Place on the baking sheets and flatten slightly. Brush each ball with a little water and sift over a thin layer of icing sugar.

4 Bake for 20–25 minutes, until just firm. With a metal spatula, transfer to a wire rack to cool completely.

Nutritional information: Energy 94kcal/393kJ; Protein 2.1g; Carbohydrate 11.6g, of which sugars 11.4g; Fat 4.7g, of which saturates 0.7g; Cholesterol 0mg; Calcium 23mg; Fibre 0.6g; Sodium 9mg.

Chocolate cinnamon tuiles

Slim, curvy and quite irresistible, these chocolate tuiles are a great accompaniment for sophisticated desserts. They are best eaten on the same day as they are made.

MAKES 12

1 egg white
50g/2oz/¹⁄₄ cup caster (superfine) sugar
30ml/2 tbsp plain (all-purpose) flour
40g/1¹⁄₂oz/3 tbsp butter, melted
15ml/1 tbsp unsweetened cocoa powder
2.5ml/¹⁄₂ tsp ground cinnamon

1 Preheat the oven to 200°C/400°F/Gas 6. Lightly grease two large baking sheets. Whisk the egg white in a clean, grease-free bowl until it forms soft peaks. Gradually whisk in the sugar to make a smooth, glossy mixture.

2 Sift the flour over the mixture and fold in. Stir in the butter. Transfer about 45ml/3 tbsp of the mixture to a small bowl and set aside. In a separate bowl, mix together the cocoa and cinnamon. Stir into the larger quantity of mixture.

3 Leaving room for spreading, drop spoonfuls of the chocolate-flavoured mixture on to the baking sheets, then spread each gently with a metal spatula to make a neat round. Using a small spoon, drizzle the reserved plain mixture over the rounds, swirling it lightly to give a marbled effect.

4 Bake for 4–6 minutes, until just set. Using a metal spatula, lift each biscuit carefully and quickly drape it over a rolling pin, to give a curved shape as it hardens. Allow the tuiles to cool until set, then remove them gently and finish cooling on a wire rack.

Nutritional information: Energy 55kcal/229kJ; Protein 0.8g; Carbohydrate 6.5g, of which sugars 4.4g; Fat 3g, of which saturates 1.9g; Cholesterol 7mg; Calcium 8mg; Fibre 0.2g; Sodium 38mg.

Cranberry and chocolate squares

Made for each other – the contrasting flavours of tangy cranberries and sweet chocolate.

MAKES 12

150g/5oz/1¼ cups self-raising (self-rising) flour, plus extra for dusting
115g/4oz/½ cup unsalted (sweet) butter
60ml/4 tbsp unsweetened cocoa powder
215g/7½oz/1¼ cups light muscovado (brown) sugar
2 eggs, beaten
115g/4oz/1 cup fresh or thawed frozen cranberries
75ml/5 tbsp grated plain (semisweet) chocolate, for sprinkling

FOR THE TOPPING

150ml/¼ pint/⅔ cup sour cream
75g/3oz/6 tbsp caster (superfine) sugar
30ml/2 tbsp self-raising (self-rising) flour
50g/2oz/4 tbsp soft margarine
1 egg, beaten
2.5ml/½ tsp vanilla extract

1 Preheat the oven to 180°C/350°F/Gas 4. Grease an 18 x 27cm/7 x 10½in cake tin (pan) and dust with flour. Put the butter, cocoa and sugar in a pan and stir over a low heat until melted and smooth. Remove from the heat and stir in the flour and eggs, beating until mixed. Stir in the cranberries, then spread into the prepared tin.

2 Make the topping by mixing all the ingredients in a bowl. Beat until smooth, then spread over the base.

3 Sprinkle with grated chocolate and bake for 40–45 minutes until risen. Cool in the tin. Cut into 12 squares.

Nutritional information: Energy 343kcal/1439kJ; Protein 4.8g; Carbohydrate 42.9g, of which sugars 30.8g; Fat 18.2g, of which saturates 8.7g; Cholesterol 76mg; Calcium 63mg; Fibre 1.4g; Sodium 164mg.

Chunky double chocolate cookies

Keep these luscious treats under lock and key, as they will disappear in a flash!

MAKES 18–20

115g/4oz/½ cup unsalted (sweet) butter, softened
115g/4oz/⅔ cup light muscovado (brown) sugar
1 egg
5ml/1 tsp vanilla extract
150g/5oz/1¼ cups self-raising (self-rising) flour
75g/3oz/¾ cup rolled oats
115g/4oz plain (semisweet) chocolate, roughly chopped
115g/4oz white chocolate, roughly chopped

1 Preheat the oven to 190°C/375°F/Gas 5. Lightly grease two baking sheets. Cream the butter with the sugar in a bowl until pale and fluffy. Add the egg and vanilla extract and beat well.

2 Sift the flour over the mixture and fold in lightly with a metal spoon, then add the oats and chopped plain and white chocolate and stir until evenly mixed.

3 Place small spoonfuls of the mixture in 18–20 rocky heaps on the baking sheets, leaving space for spreading.

4 Bake for 12–15 minutes or until the biscuits are beginning to turn pale golden. Cool for 2–3 minutes on the baking sheets, then carefully lift on to wire racks to cool completely.

Nutritional information: Energy 169kcal/710kJ; Protein 2.3g; Carbohydrate 21.6g, of which sugars 13.1g; Fat 8.8g, of which saturates 5.1g; Cholesterol 22mg; Calcium 36mg; Fibre 0.6g; Sodium 47mg.

Chunky chocolate drops

Three different types of chocolate and toasted pecan nuts make a heavenly combination.
You may need to bake these biscuits in batches. Store them in an airtight container.

MAKES ABOUT 18

175g/6oz bittersweet or plain (semisweet)
   chocolate, chopped into small pieces
115g/4oz/¹/₂ cup unsalted (sweet)
   butter, diced
2 eggs
115g/4oz/¹/₂ cup sugar
50g/2oz/¹/₃ cup soft light brown sugar
40g/1¹/₂oz/6 tbsp plain (all-purpose) flour
25g/1oz/¹/₄ cup unsweetened cocoa
   powder
5ml/1 tsp baking powder
10ml/2 tsp vanilla extract
pinch of salt
115g/4oz/1 cup pecan nuts, toasted and
   coarsely chopped
175g/6oz/1 cup plain (semisweet)
   chocolate chips
115g/4oz fine quality white chocolate,
   chopped into small pieces
115g/4oz fine quality milk chocolate,
   chopped into small pieces

1 Preheat the oven to 160°C/325°F/ Gas 3. Grease large baking sheets. Melt the chocolate and butter gently in a pan, stirring frequently, until smooth. Cool slightly.

2 In a large bowl, beat the eggs and sugars until pale and creamy. Gradually pour in the melted chocolate mixture, beating well.

3 Beat in the flour, cocoa, baking powder and vanilla extract. Stir in the remaining ingredients.

4 Drop heaped tablespoons of the mixture on to the baking sheets, 10cm/4in apart. Flatten each to a 7.5cm/3in round. (You will only get 4–6 biscuits on each sheet.)

5 Bake for 10 minutes until the tops are shiny and cracked and the edges look crisp. Do not over-bake or the biscuits will break when they are removed from the baking sheets. Allow to cool for 2 minutes until the biscuits are just set, then transfer to wire racks to cool completely.

Nutritional information: Energy 264kcal/1101kJ; Protein 3.4g; Carbohydrate 21.1g, of which sugars 20.7g; Fat 19.1g, of which saturates 9.1g; Cholesterol 37mg; Calcium 48mg; Fibre 0.9g; Sodium 73mg.

Chocolate amaretti

Crisp and flavoured with almonds, these little cookies are ideal to serve with after-dinner coffee. When toasting almonds, watch them carefully and turn them occasionally as they burn easily.

MAKES ABOUT 24

115g/4oz/1 cup blanched whole almonds
115g/4oz/1/2 cup caster (superfine) sugar
15ml/1 tbsp unsweetened cocoa powder
30ml/2 tbsp icing (confectioners') sugar
2 egg whites
pinch of cream of tartar
5ml/1 tsp almond extract
flaked (sliced) almonds, to decorate

1 Preheat the oven to 180°C/350°F/Gas 4. Place the almonds on a baking sheet and bake for 10 minutes until golden. Cool. Reduce the oven temperature to 160°C/325°F/Gas 3. Line a baking sheet with baking parchment.

2 In a food processor, process the almonds with half the caster sugar until finely ground. Transfer to a bowl and stir in the cocoa and icing sugar.

3 Whisk the egg whites and cream of tartar together in a large bowl until stiff peaks form.

4 Sprinkle in the remaining caster sugar, a little at a time, whisking after each addition, until the whites are glossy and stiff. Whisk in the almond extract. Fold the almond mixture into the egg whites.

5 Spoon into a piping bag fitted with a plain nozzle and pipe 4cm/1½in rounds on the baking sheet. Press a flaked almond on to each and bake for 15 minutes until crisp and golden.

6 Cool on the baking sheet for 10 minutes, then transfer to wire racks to cool completely before serving.

Nutritional information: Energy 65kcal/270kJ; Protein 1.8g; Carbohydrate 5.8g, of which sugars 5.5g; Fat 4g, of which saturates 0.4g; Cholesterol 0mg; Calcium 20mg; Fibre 0.6g; Sodium 12mg.

Black and white ginger florentines

As a change from the usual florentines, made with dried fruit and glacé cherries, this spicy version is wonderfully flavoured with stem ginger and candied orange peel.

MAKES ABOUT 30

120ml/4fl oz/^{1}/$_2$ cup double
  (heavy) cream
50g/2oz/^{1}/$_4$ cup butter
50g/2oz/^{1}/$_4$ cup sugar
30ml/2 tbsp honey
150g/5oz/1^1/$_4$ cups flaked
  (sliced) almonds
40g/1^1/$_2$oz/6 tbsp plain
  (all-purpose) flour

2.5ml/^{1}/$_2$ tsp ground ginger
50g/2oz/^{1}/$_3$ cup diced candied
  orange peel
75g/3oz/^{1}/$_2$ cup diced preserved
  stem ginger
50g/2oz plain (semisweet) chocolate,
  chopped into small pieces
150g/5oz dark (bittersweet) chocolate
150g/5oz white chocolate, chopped

1 Preheat the oven to 180°C/350°F/Gas 4. Lightly grease two large baking sheets. In a pan over a medium heat, stir the cream, butter, sugar and honey until the sugar dissolves. Bring the mixture to the boil, stirring constantly. Remove from the heat and stir in the almonds, flour and ground ginger. Stir in the candied peel, stem ginger and plain chocolate.

2 Drop teaspoons of the mixture on to the baking sheets at least 7.5cm/3in apart. Spread each round as thinly as possible with the back of the spoon.

3 Bake for 8–10 minutes until the edges are golden brown and the biscuits are bubbling. Do not under-bake or they will be sticky, but take care, as they burn easily. Bake in batches. If you wish, use a 7.5cm/3in cutter to neaten the edges of the florentines while still on the baking sheets.

4 Allow the biscuits to cool on the baking sheets for 10 minutes, until they are firm enough to move. Using a metal spatula, carefully lift the biscuits on to a wire rack to cool completely.

5 Melt the dark chocolate in a heatproof bowl over barely simmering water. Cool slightly. Put the white chocolate in a separate bowl and melt in the same way. Remove from the heat and cool for about 5 minutes, stirring occasionally.

6 Using a metal spatula, spread half the florentines with the dark chocolate and half with the melted white chocolate. Place on a wire rack, chocolate side up. Chill for 10–15 minutes to set.

Nutritional information: Energy 71kcal/298kJ; Protein 0.9g; Carbohydrate 8.6g, of which sugars 7.8g; Fat 3.9g, of which saturates 1.3g; Cholesterol 2mg; Calcium 16mg; Fibre 0.3g; Sodium 11mg.

Choc-chip nut biscuits

These cookies are equally delicious made with milk chocolate chips, or why not try a combination? Any version is guaranteed to be popular with children.

MAKES 36

115g/4oz/1 cup plain (all-purpose) flour
5ml/1 tsp baking powder
5ml/1 tsp salt
75g/3oz/6 tbsp butter or margarine
115g/4oz/$^{1}/_{2}$ cup caster
   (superfine) sugar
50g/2oz/$^{1}/_{3}$ cup soft light brown sugar
1 egg
5ml/1 tsp vanilla extract
115g/4oz/$^{2}/_{3}$ cup plain (semisweet)
   chocolate chips
50g/2oz/$^{1}/_{2}$ cup hazelnuts, chopped

1 Preheat the oven to 180°C/350°F/Gas 4. Grease 2–3 baking sheets. Sift the flour, baking powder and salt into a small bowl. Set the bowl aside.

2 With a hand-held electric mixer, cream the butter or margarine and sugars together in another bowl. Beat in the egg and vanilla extract. Add the flour mixture and beat well on low speed.

3 Stir in the chocolate chips and half of the hazelnuts. Drop teaspoonfuls of the mixture on to the prepared baking sheets, to form 2cm/$^{3}/_{4}$in mounds. Space the biscuits about 5cm/2in apart to allow room for spreading.

4 Flatten each biscuit lightly with a wet fork. Sprinkle the remaining hazelnuts on top of the biscuits and press lightly into the surface. Bake for 10–12 minutes, until golden brown. Transfer the biscuits to a wire rack and allow to cool.

Nutritional information: Energy 66kcal/278kJ; Protein 0.9g; Carbohydrate 7.9g, of which sugars 5.5g; Fat 3.7g, of which saturates 1.7g; Cholesterol 10mg; Calcium 10mg; Fibre 0.3g; Sodium 70mg.

Chocolate crackle-tops

These little cookies will crack slightly during baking, which creates an attractive pattern on the surface. They have a lovely rich, slightly chewy texture.

MAKES ABOUT 38

200g/7oz dark (bittersweet) or plain (semisweet) chocolate, chopped into small pieces

90g/3½oz/7 tbsp unsalted (sweet) butter

115g/4oz/½ cup caster (superfine) sugar

3 eggs

5ml/1 tsp vanilla extract

200g/7oz/1¾ cups plain (all-purpose) flour

25g/1oz/¼ cup unsweetened cocoa powder

2.5ml/½ tsp baking powder

pinch of salt

175g/6oz/1½ cups icing (confectioners') sugar, for coating

1 Grease two large baking sheets. Melt the chocolate and butter in a pan over a low heat, stirring frequently. Remove from the heat. Stir in the sugar until dissolved. Add the eggs, one at a time, beating well. Stir in the vanilla.

2 Sift the flour, cocoa, baking powder and salt into a bowl. Gradually stir into the chocolate mixture to make a soft dough. Chill for at least 1 hour until the dough is firm enough to hold its shape.

3 Preheat the oven to 160°C/325°F/Gas 3. Place the icing sugar in a bowl. Using an ice cream scoop or teaspoon, scoop the dough into small balls and roll between your palms. Drop the balls, one at a time, into the icing sugar and roll until coated. Place on the baking sheets, about 4cm/1½in apart.

4 Bake for 10–15 minutes until the top of each feels slightly firm. Leave for 2–3 minutes until just set. Transfer to wire racks and cool completely.

Nutritional information: Energy 102kcal/428kJ; Protein 1.5g; Carbohydrate 15.8g, of which sugars 11.4g; Fat 4.1g, of which saturates 2.3g; Cholesterol 20mg; Calcium 17mg; Fibre 0.4g; Sodium 27mg.

Nut and chocolate chip brownies

Moist, dark and deeply satisfying – meet the ultimate chocolate brownie. These are ideal for serving with tea and can be frozen for up to three months in an airtight container.

MAKES 16

150g/5oz plain (semisweet) chocolate, broken into squares

120ml/4fl oz/1/2 cup sunflower oil

215g/71/2oz/11/4 cups light muscovado (brown) sugar

2 eggs

5ml/1 tsp vanilla extract

65g/21/2oz/2/3 cup self-raising (self-rising) flour

60ml/4 tbsp unsweetened cocoa powder

75g/3oz/3/4 cup chopped walnuts or pecan nuts

60ml/4 tbsp milk chocolate chips

1 Preheat the oven to 180°C/350°F/Gas 4. Lightly grease a shallow 19cm/71/2in square cake tin (pan). Melt the plain chocolate in a heatproof bowl over a pan of barely simmering water.

2 Beat the oil, sugar, eggs and vanilla extract together in a large bowl. Stir in the melted chocolate, then beat well until evenly mixed and smooth.

3 Sift the flour and cocoa powder into the bowl and fold in thoroughly. Stir in the chopped nuts and chocolate chips, turn into the prepared tin and spread evenly to the edges.

4 Bake the cake in the oven for 30–35 minutes, or until the top is firm and crusty. Allow to cool in the tin before cutting into squares.

Nutritional information: Energy 235kcal/983kJ; Protein 3.4g; Carbohydrate 25.9g, of which sugars 22.2g; Fat 13.9g, of which saturates 3.8g; Cholesterol 25mg; Calcium 37mg; Fibre 1g; Sodium 49mg.

Low-fat brownies

Whether it is coffee time or a special occasion dessert, these brownies are the perfect choice.
Make sure the bananas are ripe, as under-ripe ones will be less sweet and harder to mash.

MAKES 9

75ml/5 tbsp fat-reduced cocoa powder
15ml/1 tbsp caster (superfine) sugar
75ml/5 tbsp skimmed milk
3 large bananas, mashed
175g/6oz/1 cup soft light brown sugar
5ml/1 tsp vanilla extract
5 egg whites
75g/3oz/¾ cup self-raising (self-rising) flour
75g/3oz/¾ cup oat bran
15ml/1 tbsp icing (confectioners') sugar, for dusting

1 Preheat the oven to 180°C/ 350°F/Gas 4. Line a 20cm/8in square cake tin (pan) with baking parchment.

2 Blend the cocoa powder and caster sugar with the milk in a bowl. Mix in the bananas, soft brown sugar and vanilla extract.

3 In a separate bowl, lightly beat the egg whites with a fork.

4 Add the chocolate mixture to the egg whites and continue to beat well. Sift the flour over the mixture and fold in with the oat bran. Pour the mixture into the prepared tin.

5 Bake for 40 minutes or until the top is firm and crusty. Cool in the tin before cutting into squares. Lightly dust the brownies with icing sugar before serving.

Nutritional information: Energy 101kcal/426kJ; Protein 4.6g; Carbohydrate 16.6g, of which sugars 10.8g; Fat 2.2g, of which saturates 1.2g; Cholesterol 0mg; Calcium 31mg; Fibre 2.8g; Sodium 167mg.

Marbled brownies

An alternative to the usual brownies, these contain cream cheese. Allow the brownies to cool in the tin and, when cold, carefully turn the cake out and cut into squares.

MAKES 24

225g/8oz plain (semisweet) chocolate, chopped into small pieces
75g/3oz/6 tbsp butter, diced
4 eggs
300g/11oz/scant 1¹/₂ cups sugar
150g/5oz/1¹/₄ cups plain (all-purpose) flour
2.5ml/¹/₂ tsp salt
5ml/1 tsp baking powder
10ml/2 tsp vanilla extract
115g/4oz/1 cup walnuts, chopped

FOR THE PLAIN MIXTURE

50g/2oz/¹/₄ cup butter, at room temperature
175g/6oz/³/₄ cup cream cheese
75g/3oz/6 tbsp sugar
2 eggs
25g/1oz/¹/₄ cup plain (all-purpose) flour
5ml/1 tsp vanilla extract

1 Preheat the oven to 180°C/350°F/Gas 4. Line a 33 x 23cm/13 x 9in baking tin (pan) with baking parchment. Grease the paper. Melt the chocolate and the butter in a heatproof bowl over simmering water, stirring. Leave to cool.

2 Meanwhile, beat the eggs in a bowl until light and fluffy. Gradually add the sugar and continue beating until blended. Sift over the flour, salt and baking powder and fold in gently but thoroughly.

3 Stir in the cooled chocolate mixture. Add the vanilla extract and walnuts. Measure and set aside 450ml/16fl oz/2 cups of the chocolate mixture.

4 For the plain mixture, cream the butter and cream cheese in a bowl. Add the sugar and beat well. Beat in the eggs, flour and vanilla extract. Spread the unmeasured chocolate mixture in the tin. Pour over the plain mixture. Drop spoonfuls of the reserved chocolate mixture on top.

5 With a metal spatula, swirl the mixtures to marble them. Do not blend completely. Bake for 35–45 minutes, until just set. Leave to cool in the tin, then turn out and cut into squares for serving.

Nutritional information: Energy 259kcal/1083kJ; Protein 3.8g; Carbohydrate 28.8g, of which sugars 23.1g; Fat 15.1g, of which saturates 7.1g; Cholesterol 66mg; Calcium 42mg; Fibre 0.6g; Sodium 73mg.

White chocolate brownies with macadamia topping

Brownies with a difference – a white and plain chocolate brownie mix topped with a wicked layer of milk chocolate and macadamia nuts – what more can you ask for?

SERVES 12

115g/4oz/1 cup plain (all-purpose) flour
2.5ml/¹⁄₂ tsp baking powder
pinch of salt
175g/6oz fine quality white chocolate, chopped into small pieces
115g/4oz/¹⁄₂ cup caster (superfine) sugar
115g/4oz/¹⁄₂ cup unsalted (sweet) butter, cut into small pieces
2 eggs, lightly beaten
5ml/1 tsp vanilla extract
175g/6oz plain (semisweet) chocolate chips or plain chocolate, chopped into small pieces

FOR THE TOPPING

200g/7oz milk chocolate, chopped into small pieces
175g/6oz/1¹⁄₂ cups unsalted macadamia nuts, chopped

1 Preheat the oven to 180°C/350°F/Gas 4. Grease a 23cm/9in springform tin (pan). Sift together the flour, baking powder and salt, and set aside.

2 In a medium pan over a low heat, melt the white chocolate, sugar and butter until smooth, stirring frequently. Cool slightly, then beat in the eggs and vanilla extract. Stir in the flour mixture until well blended. Stir in the chocolate chips or chopped chocolate. Spread evenly in the prepared tin.

3 Bake for 20–25 minutes, until a cake tester inserted in the centre comes out clean; do not over-bake. Remove the cake from the oven and place the tin on a heatproof surface. Sprinkle the chopped milk chocolate over the cake and return it to the oven for 1 minute.

4 Remove the cake from the oven and spread the softened chocolate over the top. Sprinkle with the macadamias and press them into the chocolate. Cool in the tin on a wire rack for 30 minutes, then chill for 1 hour, until set. Carefully remove the cake from the tin and cut into thin wedges.

Nutritional information: Energy 501kcal/2091kJ; Protein 6.4g; Carbohydrate 45.5g, of which sugars 37.9g; Fat 34g, of which saturates 15.1g; Cholesterol 57mg; Calcium 113mg; Fibre 1.6g; Sodium 143mg.

White chocolate macadamia slices

Keep these luxurious white chocolate slices for someone special who you know will really appreciate their superb rich flavour and nutty, crunchy texture.

MAKES 16

150g/5oz/1¼ cups macadamia nuts, blanched almonds or hazelnuts
400g/14oz white chocolate, broken into squares
50g/2oz/½ cup ready-to-eat dried apricots
75g/3oz/6 tbsp unsalted (sweet) butter
5ml/1 tsp vanilla extract
3 eggs
150g/5oz/scant 1 cup light muscovado (brown) sugar
115g/4oz/1 cup self-raising (self-rising) flour

1 Preheat the oven to 190°C/375°F/Gas 5. Lightly grease two 20cm/8in round sandwich cake tins (pans) and line the base of each with baking parchment.

2 Chop the nuts and half the white chocolate, making sure that the pieces are about the same size. Cut up the apricots to similar size pieces.

3 In the top of a double boiler or in a heatproof bowl over barely simmering water, melt the remaining white chocolate with the butter. Remove from the heat and stir in the vanilla extract.

4 Whisk the eggs and sugar together in a bowl until thick and pale, then pour in the melted chocolate mixture, whisking constantly.

5 Sift the flour over the mixture and fold it in evenly. Finally, stir in the nuts, chopped white chocolate and chopped dried apricots.

6 Spoon the mixture into the prepared tins and level the tops.

7 Bake for 30–35 minutes, or until the top is firm and crusty. Allow the cakes to cool in the tins before cutting each into 8 wedges.

Nutritional information: Energy 317kcal/1326kJ; Protein 4.8g; Carbohydrate 31.6g, of which sugars 26g; Fat 20g, of which saturates 8.4g; Cholesterol 46mg; Calcium 95mg; Fibre 0.9g; Sodium 97mg.

Double chocolate chip muffins

These marvellous muffins, packed with plenty of chunky dark and white chocolate chips and dusted with a light sprinkling of cocoa powder, are great served with a cup of tea or coffee.

MAKES 16

400g/14oz/3¹/₂ cups plain
   (all-purpose) flour
15ml/1 tbsp baking powder
30ml/2 tbsp unsweetened cocoa powder
115g/4oz/³/₄ cup muscovado
   (molasses) sugar
2 eggs
150ml/¹/₄ pint/²/₃ cup sour cream
150ml/¹/₄ pint/²/₃ cup milk
60ml/4 tbsp sunflower oil
175g/6oz white chocolate
175g/6oz plain (semisweet) chocolate
cocoa powder, for dusting

1 Preheat the oven to 190°C/375°F/ Gas 5. Place 16 paper muffin cases in muffin tins (pans) or deep patty tins.

2 Sift the flour, baking powder and cocoa into a bowl and stir in the sugar. Make a well in the centre.

3 In a separate bowl, beat the eggs with the sour cream, milk and oil, then stir into the well in the dry ingredients.

4 Beat well, gradually incorporating the flour mixture to make a thick and creamy batter.

5 Chop the white and the plain chocolate into small pieces, then stir into the batter mixture. Spoon into the muffin cases, filling them almost to the top. Bake for 25–30 minutes or until well risen and firm. Allow to cool on a wire rack, then dust with cocoa powder before serving.

Nutritional information: Energy 281kcal/1183kJ; Protein 4.7g; Carbohydrate 41.3g, of which sugars 21.9g; Fat 11.9g, of which saturates 5.7g; Cholesterol 7mg; Calcium 94mg; Fibre 1.3g; Sodium 40mg.

Chocolate kisses

Made with both white and dark chocolate, and with a light dusting of icing sugar, these scrumptious morsels will prove to be love at first sight.

MAKES 24

75g/3oz dark (bittersweet) chocolate, chopped into small pieces

75g/3oz white chocolate, chopped into small pieces

115g/4oz/½ cup butter, softened

115g/4oz/½ cup caster (superfine) sugar

2 eggs

225g/8oz/2 cups plain (all-purpose) flour

icing (confectioners') sugar, to decorate

1 Melt the plain and white chocolates in separate bowls over barely simmering water and set both aside to cool.

2 Beat the butter and caster sugar together until pale and fluffy. Beat in the eggs, one at a time. Then sift in the flour and mix well.

3 Halve the creamed mixture and divide it between the two bowls of chocolate. Mix each chocolate in thoroughly so that each forms a dough. Knead the doughs until smooth, wrap them separately in clear film (plastic wrap) and chill for 1 hour. Preheat the oven to 190°C/375°F/Gas 5.

4 Shape slightly rounded teaspoonfuls of both doughs roughly into balls. Roll the balls between your palms to neaten them. Arrange the balls on greased baking sheets and bake for 10–12 minutes, until firm. Dust with sifted icing sugar and cool on a wire rack.

Nutritional information: Energy 125kcal/524kJ; Protein 1.9g; Carbohydrate 16.1g, of which sugars 9g; Fat 6.4g, of which saturates 3.7g; Cholesterol 26mg; Calcium 28mg; Fibre 0.4g; Sodium 39mg.

Chocolate fairy cakes

Always a favourite for parties, these temptingly sweet fairy cakes, with a rich, vanilla-flavoured icing, will appeal to old and young alike. For variation, try adding sprinkles or chocolate buttons.

MAKES 24

115g/4oz plain (semisweet) chocolate, chopped into small pieces
15ml/1 tbsp water
275g/10oz/2¹/₂ cups plain (all-purpose) flour
5ml/1 tsp baking powder
2.5ml/¹/₂ tsp bicarbonate of soda (baking soda)
pinch of salt
300g/11oz/scant 1¹/₂ cups caster (superfine) sugar
175g/6oz/³/₄ cup butter or margarine
150ml/¹/₄ pint/²/₃ cup milk
5ml/1 tsp vanilla extract
3 eggs

FOR THE ICING

40g/1¹/₂ oz/3 tbsp butter
115g/4oz/1 cup icing (confectioners') sugar
2.5ml/¹/₂ tsp vanilla extract
15–30ml/1–2 tbsp milk

1 Preheat the oven to 180°C/350°F/Gas 4. Grease 24 bun tins (pans), about 6.5cm/2³/₄in in diameter, and line with paper cases.

2 For the icing, soften the butter. Place it in a bowl and stir in the icing sugar, a little at a time. Add the vanilla extract, then, a drop at a time, beat in just enough milk to make a creamy, spreadable mixture. Cover and set aside.

3 Melt the chocolate and water in a heatproof bowl over simmering water. Remove from the heat. Sift the flour, baking powder, bicarbonate of soda, salt and sugar into a large bowl. Add the chocolate mixture, butter or margarine, milk and vanilla extract. With a hand-held electric mixer on medium, beat until smooth. Increase the speed to high and beat for 2 minutes. Add the eggs, one at a time, and beat for 1 minute after each addition. Divide among the tins.

4 Bake for 20–25 minutes or until a skewer inserted into the centre of a cake comes out clean. Cool in the tins for 10 minutes, then turn out to cool completely on a wire rack. Spread the top of each cake with the icing, swirling it into a peak in the centre.

Nutritional information: Energy 228kcal/957kJ; Protein 2.5g; Carbohydrate 30.6g, of which sugars 21g; Fat 11.5g, of which saturates 3.3g; Cholesterol 33mg; Calcium 40mg; Fibre 0.5g; Sodium 95mg.

Chocolate raspberry macaroon bars

A perfect match – rich chocolate taste with the bite of raspberries and the crunch of almonds. Save these for a rainy day and savour the melt-in-the-mouth flavours.

MAKES 16–18 BARS

115g/4oz/½ cup unsalted (sweet) butter, softened
50g/2oz/½ cup icing (confectioners') sugar
25g/1oz/¼ cup unsweetened cocoa powder
pinch of salt
5ml/1 tsp almond extract
115g/4oz/1 cup plain (all-purpose) flour

FOR THE TOPPING

150g/5oz/½ cup seedless raspberry jam
15ml/1 tbsp raspberry-flavoured liqueur
175g/6oz/1 cup mini chocolate chips
175g/6oz/1½ cups ground almonds
4 egg whites
pinch of salt
225g/8oz/1 cup caster (superfine) sugar
2.5ml/½ tsp almond extract
50g/2oz/¼ cup flaked (sliced) almonds

1 Preheat the oven to 160°C/325°F/Gas 3. Invert a 33 x 23cm/13 x 9in baking tin (pan). Mould a sheet of foil over the tin and smooth around the corners. Lift off and turn the tin right side up; line with the moulded foil, then grease.

2 Beat the butter, sugar, cocoa powder and salt with a hand-held electric mixer for about 1 minute, until blended and creamy. Beat in the almond extract and the flour until it forms a crumbly dough. Turn into the prepared tin and even out. Prick the dough with a fork. Bake for 20 minutes until the pastry has set. Remove from the oven and increase the temperature to 190°C/375°F/Gas 5.

3 For the topping, combine the raspberry jam and the liqueur in a bowl. Spread evenly over the chocolate crust, then sprinkle with the chocolate chips. In a food processor fitted with a metal blade, process the ground almonds, egg whites, salt, sugar and almond extract until well blended and foamy. Gently pour over the jam layer, spreading to the edges of the tin. Sprinkle with the flaked almonds. Bake for 20 minutes more, until golden and puffed.

4 Cool in the tin for 20 minutes, until firm. Using the edges of the foil, carefully remove from the tin and cool completely. Peel off the foil and cut into bars.

Nutritional information: Energy 266kcal/1115kJ; Protein 4.5g; Carbohydrate 32.1g, of which sugars 26.6g; Fat 14.1g, of which saturates 5.7g; Cholesterol 16mg; Calcium 66mg; Fibre 1.2g; Sodium 79mg.

Chocolate pecan squares

The chopped pecan nuts in these tasty squares add a wonderfully crunchy texture – this is a delicious variation on the traditional chocolate brownie.

MAKES 16

2 eggs
10ml/2 tsp vanilla extract
pinch of salt
175g/6oz/1½ cups pecan nuts,
    roughly chopped
50g/2oz/½ cup plain (all-purpose) flour
50g/2oz/¼ cup sugar
120ml/4fl oz/½ cup golden
    (light corn) syrup
75g/3oz plain (semisweet) chocolate,
    chopped into small pieces
40g/1½oz/3 tbsp unsalted
    (sweet) butter
16 pecan nut halves, to decorate

1 Preheat the oven to 160°C/325°F/Gas 3. Line a 20cm/8in square baking tin with baking parchment. Whisk the eggs with the vanilla extract and salt. In another bowl, mix together the pecan nuts and flour.

2 Put the sugar in a pan, add the golden syrup and bring to the boil. Remove from the heat and stir in the chocolate and butter until the mixture is smooth.

3 Stir the egg mixture into the chocolate mixture, then fold in the pecan nuts and flour. Pour into the prepared tin and bake for about 35 minutes or until firm to the touch.

4 Allow to cool in the tin for 10 minutes before turning out on a wire rack. Cut into 5cm/2in squares and press pecan halves into the tops while still warm. Cool completely before serving.

Nutritional information: Energy 194kcal/808kJ; Protein 2.7g; Carbohydrate 15.4g, of which sugars 12.8g; Fat 14g, of which saturates 3.1g; Cholesterol 29mg; Calcium 21mg; Fibre 0.9g; Sodium 45mg.

Chocolate butterscotch bars

Unashamedly rich and sweet, these bars are perfect for chocoholics of all ages. Make sure the chocolate topping is set before cutting into bars.

MAKES 24

225g/8oz/2 cups plain (all-purpose) flour
2.5ml/$\frac{1}{2}$ tsp baking powder
115g/4oz/$\frac{1}{2}$ cup unsalted (sweet) butter
50g/2oz/$\frac{1}{3}$ cup light muscovado (brown) sugar
150g/5oz plain (semisweet) chocolate, melted
30ml/2 tbsp ground almonds

FOR THE TOPPING

175g/6oz/$\frac{3}{4}$ cup unsalted (sweet) butter
115g/4oz/$\frac{1}{2}$ cup caster (superfine) sugar
30ml/2 tbsp golden (light corn) syrup
175ml/6fl oz/$\frac{3}{4}$ cup sweetened condensed milk
150g/5oz/$1\frac{1}{4}$ cups whole toasted hazelnuts
225g/8oz plain (semisweet) chocolate, broken into squares

1 Preheat the oven to 160°C/325°F/Gas 3. Lightly grease a shallow 30 x 20cm/12 x 8in tin (pan). Sift the flour and baking powder into a large bowl.

2 Rub in the butter until the mixture resembles coarse breadcrumbs, then stir in the sugar. Work in the melted chocolate and ground almonds to make a well blended dough.

3 Press the dough into the tin, prick with a fork and bake for 25–30 minutes until firm. Leave to cool in the tin.

4 For the topping, place the butter, sugar, golden syrup and condensed milk in a pan. Heat gently, stirring, until the butter and sugar have melted. Simmer, stirring, until golden, then stir in the hazelnuts. Pour over the cooked base and leave to set.

5 Melt the chocolate in a heatproof bowl over barely simmering water. Spread the melted chocolate over the butterscotch layer, then leave to set before cutting into bars to serve.

Nutritional information: Energy 305kcal/1273kJ; Protein 3.5g; Carbohydrate 30g, of which sugars 22.5g; Fat 19.8g, of which saturates 9.7g; Cholesterol 29mg; Calcium 57mg; Fibre 1.2g; Sodium 89mg.

Chocolate cinnamon doughnuts

Just as tempting as traditional jam doughnuts, these light and luscious treats are best served freshly made and just warm, so that the chocolate filling really melts in your mouth.

MAKES 16

500g/1¼lb/5 cups strong white
    bread flour
30ml/2 tbsp unsweetened cocoa powder
2.5ml/½ tsp salt
1 sachet easy-blend (rapid-rise)
    dried yeast
300ml/½ pint/1¼ cups hand-hot milk

40g/1½oz/3 tbsp butter, melted
1 egg, beaten
115g/4oz plain (semisweet) chocolate,
    broken into 16 pieces
sunflower oil, for deep-frying

FOR THE COATING
45ml/3 tbsp caster (superfine) sugar
15ml/1 tbsp unsweetened cocoa powder
5ml/1 tsp ground cinnamon

1 Sift the flour, cocoa and salt into a bowl. Stir in the yeast. Make a well in the centre and add the milk, melted butter and egg. Stir, incorporating the dry ingredients to make a soft and pliable dough.

2 Knead the dough on a lightly floured surface for about 5 minutes, or until smooth and elastic.

3 Return to the clean bowl, cover and leave in a warm place until the dough has doubled in bulk.

4 Knead the dough lightly again on a floured surface, then divide into 16 pieces. Shape each piece into a round and press a piece of chocolate into the centre. Fold the dough over to enclose, pressing firmly to seal.

5 Heat the oil to 180°C/350°F or until a cube of bread browns in 30 seconds. Deep-fry the doughnuts in batches. As each doughnut rises and turns golden brown, turn it over to cook the other side. Drain well on kitchen paper.

6 Mix the sugar, cocoa and cinnamon. Toss the doughnuts in the mixture to coat them evenly. Serve warm.

Nutritional information: Energy 235kcal/989kJ; Protein 5.1g; Carbohydrate 33.2g, of which sugars 9g; Fat 10.1g, of which saturates 2.7g; Cholesterol 14mg; Calcium 76mg; Fibre 1.5g; Sodium 48mg.

Brioches au chocolat

Steal out of bed early and surprise the one you love with these wonderful French specialities. Light, golden and drizzled with melted chocolate, they are bound to go down well.

MAKES 12

250g/9oz/2¼ cups strong white
    bread flour
pinch of salt
30ml/2 tbsp caster (superfine) sugar
1 sachet easy-blend (rapid-rise)
    dried yeast
3 eggs, beaten, plus extra beaten egg,
    for glazing
45ml/3 tbsp hand-hot milk
115g/4oz/½ cup unsalted (sweet)
    butter, diced
175g/6oz plain (semisweet)
    chocolate, broken into squares, plus
    extra, for drizzling

1 Sift the flour, salt and sugar into a large bowl and stir in the yeast. Make a well in the centre of the mixture and add the eggs and milk.

2 Beat well, gradually incorporating the surrounding dry ingredients to make a soft dough. Turn on to a lightly floured surface and knead until smooth and elastic, adding a little more flour if necessary.

3 Add the butter to the dough, a few pieces at a time, kneading until each addition is absorbed before adding the next. When all the butter has been incorporated and small bubbles appear in the dough, wrap it in clear film (plastic wrap)and chill for at least 1 hour, or overnight.

4 Grease 12 individual brioche tins (pans) set on a baking sheet or a 12-hole brioche or patty tin (muffin pan).

5 Divide the dough into 12 pieces and shape each into a smooth round. Place a chocolate square in the centre. Bring up the sides of the dough and press the edges firmly together to seal.

6 Place the brioches, join side down, in the prepared tins. Cover and leave them in a warm place for about 30 minutes or until doubled in size.

7 Preheat the oven to 200°C/400°F/ Gas 6. Brush the brioches with beaten egg and bake for 12–15 minutes until well risen and golden.

8 Place on wire racks and leave until warm. Melt the remaining chocolate in a heatproof bowl set over a pan of simmering water and drizzle over the brioches. Serve immediately.

Nutritional information: Energy 236kcal/ 988kJ; Protein 4.3g; Carbohydrate 27g, of which sugars 11g; Fat 13.1g, of which saturates 7.6g; Cholesterol 69mg; Calcium 48mg; Fibre 1g; Sodium 79mg.

Chocolate mint-filled cupcakes

Chocolate on chocolate – what could be better? Mint, of course! This classic taste combination, with its creamy mint filling and glaze, will have you coming back for seconds.

MAKES 12

225g/8oz/2 cups plain (all-purpose) flour

5ml/1 tsp bicarbonate of soda
  (baking soda)

pinch of salt

50g/2oz/½ cup unsweetened cocoa
  powder

150g/5oz/10 tbsp unsalted (sweet)
  butter, softened

350g/12oz/1½ cups caster (superfine)
  sugar

3 eggs

5ml/1 tsp peppermint extract

250ml/8 fl oz/1 cup milk

FOR THE MINT CREAM FILLING

300ml/½ pint/1¼ cups whipping cream

5ml/1 tsp peppermint extract

FOR THE CHOCOLATE
MINT GLAZE

175g/6oz plain (semisweet) chocolate,
  roughly chopped

115g/4oz/½ cup unsalted
  (sweet) butter

5ml/1 tsp peppermint extract

1 Preheat the oven to 180°C/350°F/ Gas 4. Line a 12-hole patty tin (muffin pan) with paper cases. Sift the flour, bicarbonate of soda, salt and cocoa powder into a bowl. In a separate bowl, whisk the butter and sugar together for 5 minutes until light and creamy. Add the eggs, one at a time, whisking after each addition.

2 Beat in the peppermint extract. With the whisk, beat in the flour-cocoa mixture alternately with the milk, until blended. Spoon into the paper cases. Bake for 15 minutes, or until a skewer inserted in the centre comes out clean. Cool on a wire rack.

3 When cool, carefully remove the paper cases. For the mint cream filling, whip the cream and peppermint extract until stiff. Fit a small, plain nozzle into a piping bag and spoon in the flavoured cream.

4 Press the nozzle into the bottom of each cupcake, squeezing gently to release 15ml/1 tbsp of the cream into the centre.

5 For the glaze, gently melt the chocolate and butter in a pan, stirring until smooth. Remove from the heat and stir in the peppermint extract. Cool, then spread on top of the cakes.

Nutritional information: Energy 438kcal/1829kJ; Protein 5.1g; Carbohydrate 42.5g, of which sugars 30.3g; Fat 28.7g, of which saturates 17.5g; Cholesterol 101mg; Calcium 82mg; Fibre 1.2g; Sodium 171mg.

Chocolate-orange Battenberg

This attractively presented geometric cake, with its wrapping of white almond paste and hint of orange, makes a tasty, bite-sized afternoon snack.

SERVES 8

115g/4oz/¹/₂ cup soft margarine
115g/4oz/¹/₂ cup caster (superfine) sugar
2 eggs, beaten
few drops of vanilla extract
115g/4oz/1 cup ground almonds
115g/4oz/1 cup self-raising
    (self-rising) flour

grated rind and juice of ¹/₂ orange
30ml/2 tbsp unsweetened cocoa
    powder
30–45ml/2–3 tbsp milk
1 jar chocolate and nut spread
cornflour (cornstarch), for dusting
225g/8oz white almond paste

1 Preheat the oven to 180°C/350°F/Gas 4. Grease and line an 18cm/7in square cake tin (pan). Arrange a double piece of foil across the middle of the tin, to divide it into two equal rectangles.

2 Cream the margarine and sugar in a mixing bowl, then beat in the eggs, vanilla extract and ground almonds. Divide the mixture evenly between two bowls. Sift half the flour into one bowl, fold in, then stir in the orange rind and sufficient juice to give a soft dropping (pourable) consistency. Set the orange-flavoured mixture aside.

3 Sift the rest of the flour and the cocoa into the remaining bowl of mixture, fold in, then stir in sufficient milk to give a soft dropping consistency. Fill one half of the tin with the orange mixture and the second half with the chocolate. Flatten the top with a wetted spoon. Bake for 15 minutes, then reduce the heat to 160°C/325°F/Gas 3, and bake the cake for a further 20–30 minutes or until the top is just firm. Leave to cool in the tin for a few minutes. Turn out the cakes on to a board and cut each one into two identical strips. Trim so that they are even, then leave to cool.

4 Using the chocolate and nut spread, sandwich the cakes together, chocolate and orange side by side, then orange and chocolate on top. Spread the sides with more of the chocolate and nut spread. On a board lightly dusted with cornflour, roll out the white almond paste to a rectangle 18cm/7in wide and long enough to wrap all around the cake.

5 Wrap the almond paste carefully around the cake, making the join underneath. Press to seal. Mark a criss-cross pattern on the almond paste with a knife, then pinch together the corners if desired. Store in a cool place. Cut with a sharp knife into chequered slices to serve.

Nutritional information: Energy 716kcal/2993kJ; Protein 11.5g; Carbohydrate 77.2g, of which sugars 65g; Fat 42.3g, of which saturates 6.9g; Cholesterol 49mg; Calcium 163mg; Fibre 2.9g; Sodium 204mg.

Large cakes and loaves

There can be few people who would turn down a slice of chocolate sponge cake; think how they'll react when you put a slice of Frosted Chocolate Fudge Cake in front of them. If you need a cake for a special occasion, then nothing could be more indulgent than a lavish Sachertorte or a very rich Death by Chocolate cake.

Chocolate almond mousse cake

Part cake, part mousse, surrender to a taste sensation with the superb combination of chocolate and almonds. Serve chilled for the perfect after-dinner treat.

SERVES 8

50g/2oz dark (bittersweet) chocolate,
   broken into squares
200g/7oz marzipan, grated or chopped
200ml/7fl oz/scant 1 cup milk
115g/4oz/1 cup self-raising (self-rising)
   flour
2 eggs, separated
75g/3oz/^{1}/$_2$ cup light muscovado
   (brown) sugar

FOR THE MOUSSE FILLING

115g/4oz plain (semisweet) chocolate,
   broken into squares
50g/2oz/4 tbsp unsalted (sweet) butter
2 eggs, separated
30ml/2 tbsp Amaretto di Sarone liqueur

FOR THE TOPPING

1 quantity Chocolate Ganache
toasted flaked (sliced) almonds

1 Preheat the oven to 190°C/375°F/Gas 5. Grease a deep 17cm/6^1/$_2$in square cake tin (pan) and line with baking parchment. Combine the chocolate, marzipan and milk in a pan and heat gently, stirring until melted and smooth. Sift the flour into a bowl and add the chocolate mixture and egg yolks, beating until evenly mixed.

2 Whisk the egg whites in a clean, grease-free bowl until stiff enough to hold firm peaks. Whisk in the sugar gradually. Stir about 15ml/1 tbsp of the whites into the chocolate mixture, then fold in the rest. Spoon the mixture into the tin, spreading it evenly. Bake for 45–50 minutes, until well risen, firm and springy to the touch. Remove from the tin and leave to cool on a wire rack.

3 For the mousse filling, melt the chocolate and butter in a heatproof bowl set over simmering water. Remove from the heat and beat in the egg yolks and Amaretto. Whisk the egg whites in a clean, grease-free bowl until stiff, then fold into the chocolate mixture. Slice the cold cake in half across the middle to make two layers. Return one half to the clean tin and pour over the mousse. Top with the second layer of cake and press down lightly. Chill until set.

4 Turn the cake out on to a serving plate. Spread the chocolate ganache over the top and sides, then press toasted flaked almonds over the sides. Serve chilled.

Nutritional information: Energy 420kcal/1766kJ; Protein 10g; Carbohydrate 55.4g, of which sugars 44.1g; Fat 18.7g, of which saturates 8.5g; Cholesterol 117mg; Calcium 99mg; Fibre 1.6g; Sodium 160mg.

Frosted chocolate fudge cake

Rich and dreamy, with an irresistibly rich and glossy chocolate fudge frosting, this cake couldn't be easier to make, and more wonderful to eat! Perfect for a special occasion.

SERVES 6–8

115g/4oz plain (semisweet) chocolate, broken into squares

175g/6oz/¾ cup unsalted (sweet) butter or margarine, softened

200g/7oz/generous 1 cup light muscovado (brown) sugar

5ml/1 tsp vanilla extract

3 eggs, beaten

150ml/¼ pint/⅔ cup Greek (US strained plain) yogurt

150g/5oz/1¼ cups self-raising (self-rising) flour

icing (confectioners') sugar and chocolate curls, to decorate

FOR THE FROSTING

115g/4oz dark (bittersweet) chocolate, broken into squares

50g/2oz/4 tbsp unsalted (sweet) butter

350g/12oz/3 cups icing (confectioners') sugar

90ml/6 tbsp Greek (US strained plain) yogurt

1 Preheat the oven to 190°C/ 375°F/Gas 5. Grease two 20cm/ 8in round sandwich cake tins (pans) and line the base of each tin with baking parchment.

2 Melt the chocolate gently in a heatproof bowl set over a pan of simmering water.

3 Cream the butter or margarine with the sugar until light and fluffy. Beat in the vanilla extract, then gradually add the beaten eggs, beating well after each addition. Stir in the melted chocolate and yogurt evenly. Fold in the flour with a metal spoon.

4 Divide the mixture between the tins. Bake for 30 minutes or until the cakes are firm to the touch. Turn out and cool on a wire rack.

5 For the frosting, melt the chocolate and butter in a pan over a low heat. Remove from the heat and stir in the icing sugar and yogurt.

6 Mix well, then beat until the frosting begins to cool and thicken slightly. Use a third of the frosting to sandwich the cakes together. Spread the remainder over the top and sides. Sprinkle with icing sugar and decorate with chocolate curls.

Nutritional information: Energy 753kcal/3160kJ; Protein 8g; Carbohydrate 105.4g, of which sugars 90.9g; Fat 36.6g, of which saturates 21.7g; Cholesterol 133mg; Calcium 133mg; Fibre 1.3g; Sodium 224mg.

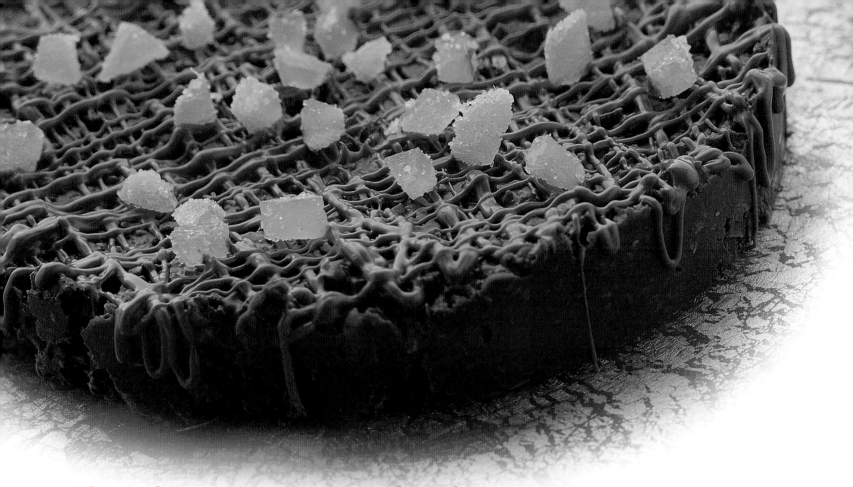

Chocolate ginger crunch cake

Ginger adds a flicker of fire to this delectable uncooked cake. Keep one in the refrigerator for spontaneous midnight feasts and other late-night treats.

SERVES 6

150g/5oz plain (semisweet) chocolate, broken into squares

50g/2oz/4 tbsp unsalted (sweet) butter

115g/4oz ginger nut biscuits (gingersnaps)

4 pieces preserved stem ginger

30ml/2 tbsp stem ginger syrup

45ml/3 tbsp desiccated (dry unsweetened shredded) coconut

TO DECORATE

25g/1oz milk chocolate

pieces of crystallized ginger

1 Grease a 15cm/6in flan tin (pan); place it on a sheet of baking parchment. Melt the plain chocolate with the butter in a heatproof bowl over barely simmering water. Remove from the heat.

2 Crush the biscuits into small pieces with a rolling pin, then put them in a bowl.

3 Chop the stem ginger fairly finely and mix with the crushed ginger nut biscuits.

4 Stir the biscuit mixture, ginger syrup and coconut into the melted chocolate and butter, mixing well until evenly combined.

5 Turn the mixture into the prepared flan tin and press down firmly and evenly. Chill until set.

6 Remove the flan ring and slide the cake on to a plate. Melt the milk chocolate, drizzle it over the top and decorate with the pieces of crystallized ginger.

Nutritional information: Energy 298kcal/1251kJ; Protein 29.1g; Carbohydrate 18.5g, of which sugars 10.2g; Fat 12.5g, of which saturates 2.3g; Cholesterol 118mg; Calcium 48mg; Fibre 4.5g; Sodium 206mg.

Chocolate brandy snap gateau

This rich, moist cake has a wonderful contrast of textures, with its crunchy, buttery brandy snap topping. It's best served straight away, otherwise the brandy snaps will go soft.

SERVES 8

225g/8oz dark (bittersweet) chocolate, broken into squares

225g/8oz/1 cup unsalted (sweet) butter, softened

200g/7oz/generous 1 cup dark muscovado (molasses) sugar

6 eggs, separated

5ml/1 tsp vanilla extract

150g/5oz/1¼ cups ground hazelnuts

60ml/4 tbsp fresh white breadcrumbs

finely grated rind of 1 large orange

1 quantity Chocolate Ganache, for filling and frosting

icing (confectioners') sugar, for dusting

FOR THE BRANDY SNAPS

50g/2oz/4 tbsp unsalted (sweet) butter

50g/2oz/¼ cup caster (superfine) sugar

75g/3oz/⅓ cup golden (light corn) syrup

50g/2oz/½ cup plain (all-purpose) flour

5ml/1 tsp brandy

1 Preheat the oven to 180°C/350°F/Gas 4. Grease two 20cm/8in sandwich cake tins (pans) and line the base of each with baking parchment. Melt the chocolate in a heatproof bowl set over a pan of simmering water. Remove from the heat.

2 Cream the butter with the sugar in a large bowl until pale and fluffy. Beat in the egg yolks and vanilla extract. Add the chocolate and mix thoroughly.

3 In a clean, grease-free bowl, whisk the egg whites until they form soft peaks, then gently fold them into the chocolate mixture with the ground hazelnuts, breadcrumbs and orange rind.

4 Divide the cake mixture equally between the two tins and level the tops. Bake for 25–30 minutes until they are risen and firm. Turn out on to wire racks.

5 To make the brandy snaps, line two large baking sheets with baking parchment. Heat the butter, sugar and syrup gently in a pan, stirring occasionally until smooth. Remove from the heat and stir in the flour and brandy.

6 Place small spoonfuls of the brandy mixture, spaced well apart, on the baking sheets and bake for 10–15 minutes until golden. Allow to cool for a few seconds until they are firm enough to lift on to a wire rack.

7 Immediately pinch the edges of each brandy snap to make a frilled effect and leave to set.

8 Sandwich the cake layers together with half the chocolate ganache, transfer to a plate and spread the remaining ganache on top.

9 Arrange the brandy snap frills over the gateau and dust with icing sugar.

Nutritional information: Energy 870kcal/3622kJ; Protein 10.7g; Carbohydrate 70g, of which sugars 59g; Fat 62.7g, of which saturates 31.2g; Cholesterol 244mg; Calcium 102mg; Fibre 2.3g; Sodium 424mg.

Sachertorte

Rich and dark, with a wonderful flavour, this glorious gateau was created in Vienna in 1832 by Franz Sacher, a chef in the royal household. Serve it with whipped cream if you wish.

SERVES 10–12

225g/8oz dark (bittersweet) chocolate,
    broken into squares
150g/5oz/²/₃ cup unsalted (sweet)
    butter, softened
115g/4oz/¹/₂ cup caster (superfine)
    sugar
8 eggs, separated
115g/4oz/1 cup plain (all-purpose) flour
plain (semisweet) chocolate curls,
    to decorate

FOR THE GLAZE
225g/8oz/1 cup apricot jam
15ml/1 tbsp lemon juice

FOR THE ICING
225g/8oz dark (bittersweet) chocolate,
    broken into squares
200g/7oz/scant 1 cup caster
    (superfine) sugar
15ml/1 tbsp golden (light corn) syrup
250ml/8fl oz/1 cup double (heavy) cream
5ml/1 tsp vanilla extract

1 Preheat the oven to 180°C/350°F/Gas 4. Grease a 23cm/9in round springform cake tin (pan) and line with baking parchment. Melt the chocolate in a heatproof bowl over a pan of simmering water.

2 Cream the butter and sugar until pale and fluffy, then beat in the egg yolks, one at a time. Beat in the chocolate, then sift the flour over and fold it in.

3 Whisk the egg whites in a clean bowl until stiff, then stir a quarter of the whites into the chocolate mixture. Fold in the remaining whites. Pour into the tin and level the top. Bake for 50–55 minutes until firm, then turn out on to a wire rack to cool.

4 For the glaze, heat the jam with the lemon juice in a pan until melted, then press through a sieve (strainer) into a bowl. Slice the cold cake in half across the middle to make two layers. Brush the top and sides of each layer with the glaze, then sandwich them together. Place on a wire rack.

5 Heat all the ingredients for the icing gently, stirring, until the mixture is thick and smooth. Simmer for 3–4 minutes until the mixture registers 95°C/200°F on a sugar thermometer. Pour the icing over the cake, spreading to cover the top and sides. Leave to set, decorate with curls and serve.

Nutritional information: Energy 625kcal/2618kJ; Protein 7.6g; Carbohydrate 73.1g, of which sugars 65.5g; Fat 35.8g, of which saturates 20.8g; Cholesterol 184mg; Calcium 73mg; Fibre 1.2g; Sodium 143mg.

Chocolate redcurrant torte

This flavoursome torte, with just the right amount of sour cream to add a rich texture, makes the perfect accompaniment to a strong cup of coffee, for an exquisite afternoon break.

SERVES 8–10

150g/5oz/1¼ cups self-raising (self-rising) flour, plus extra for dusting

115g/4oz/½ cup unsalted (sweet) butter, softened

115g/4oz/⅔ cup dark muscovado (molasses) sugar

2 eggs

150ml/¼ pint/⅔ cup sour cream

5ml/1 tsp baking powder

45ml/3 tbsp unsweetened cocoa powder

75g/3oz/¾ cup stemmed redcurrants, plus 115g/4oz/1 cup redcurrant sprigs, to decorate

FOR THE ICING

150g/5oz plain (semisweet) chocolate, broken into squares

45ml/3 tbsp redcurrant jelly

30ml/2 tbsp dark rum

120ml/4fl oz/½ cup double (heavy) cream

1 Preheat the oven to 180°C/350°F/Gas 4. Grease a 1.2-litre/2-pint/5-cup ring tin (pan) and dust lightly with flour. Cream the butter with the sugar in a mixing bowl until pale and fluffy. Beat in the eggs and sour cream until thoroughly mixed.

2 Sift the flour, baking powder and cocoa over the mixture, then fold in lightly and evenly. Fold in the stemmed redcurrants. Spoon the mixture into the prepared tin and smooth the surface level. Bake for 40 minutes or until well risen and firm.

3 Turn out on to a wire rack and leave to cool completely.

4 Make the icing. Mix the chocolate, redcurrant jelly and rum in a heatproof bowl. Set the bowl over simmering water and heat gently, stirring occasionally, until melted. Remove from the heat and stir in the cream.

5 Transfer the cooked cake to a serving plate. Spoon the icing evenly over the cake, allowing it to drizzle down the sides. Decorate with redcurrant sprigs just before serving.

Nutritional information: Energy 347kcal/1444kJ; Protein 3.7g; Carbohydrate 26.5g, of which sugars 25.9g; Fat 25.2g, of which saturates 15.3g; Cholesterol 89mg; Calcium 50mg; Fibre 1.2g; Sodium 138mg.

Chocolate date torte

This sweet and sticky torte, drizzled with melted chocolate, is best eaten on the day it is made, cut into wedges, and served with hot tea.

SERVES 8

4 egg whites
115g/4oz/¹/₂ cup caster (superfine) sugar
200g/7oz plain (semisweet) chocolate
175g/6oz/scant 1 cup Medjool dates, pitted and finely chopped
175g/6oz/1¹/₂ cups walnuts or pecan nuts, chopped
5ml/1 tsp vanilla extract

FOR THE FROSTING
200g/7oz/scant 1 cup fromage frais or cream cheese
200g/7oz/scant 1 cup mascarpone
few drops of vanilla extract
icing (confectioners') sugar, to taste

1 Preheat oven to 180°C/350°F/Gas 4. Grease a round 20cm/8in springform cake tin (pan). Line the base with baking parchment. For the frosting, mix the fromage frais or cream cheese and mascarpone together, add the vanilla extract and icing sugar to taste, then set aside.

2 Whisk the egg whites in a bowl until stiff peaks form. Whisk in 30ml/2 tbsp of the caster sugar until thick and glossy. Fold in the remainder.

3 Chop 175g/6oz of the chocolate, then fold into the meringue with the dates, nuts and vanilla extract. Pour into the tin, and bake for 45 minutes until risen around the edges. Cool in the tin for 10 minutes, then invert on a wire rack. Peel off the lining paper and leave until cold.

4 Swirl the frosting over the top. Melt the remaining chocolate. Use a small paper piping bag to drizzle the chocolate over the torte. Chill before serving.

Nutritional information: Energy 427kcal/1784kJ; Protein 9.2g; Carbohydrate 41.5g, of which sugars 40.9g; Fat 26g, of which saturates 7.8g; Cholesterol 12mg; Calcium 57mg; Fibre 2.1g; Sodium 41mg.

Meringue pyramid with chocolate mascarpone

Roses spell romance for this impressive cake. It makes the perfect centrepiece for a celebration buffet table, and most of the preparation can be done in advance.

SERVES ABOUT 10

4 egg whites

pinch of salt

175g/6oz/¾ cup caster (superfine) sugar

5ml/1 tsp ground cinnamon

75g/3oz dark (bittersweet) chocolate, grated

icing (confectioners') sugar and rose petals, to decorate

FOR THE FILLING

115g/4oz plain (semisweet) chocolate, broken into squares

5ml/1 tsp vanilla extract or rosewater

115g/4oz/½ cup mascarpone

1 Preheat the oven to 150°C/300°F/Gas 2. Line two large baking sheets with baking parchment. Whisk the egg whites with the salt in a clean, grease-free bowl until they form stiff peaks. Gradually whisk in half the sugar, then add the rest and whisk until the meringue is very stiff and glossy. Add the cinnamon and chocolate and whisk lightly to mix.

2 Draw a 20cm/8in circle on the lining paper on one of the baking sheets, replace it upside down, and spread the marked circle evenly with about half the meringue. Spoon the remaining meringue in 28–30 small neat heaps on both baking sheets. Bake for 1–1½ hours, or until crisp.

3 Make the filling. Melt the chocolate in a heatproof bowl over barely simmering water. Cool slightly, then add the vanilla extract, or rosewater, and cheese. Cool the mixture until it holds its shape.

4 Spoon the chocolate mixture into a large piping bag and sandwich the meringues together in pairs, reserving a small amount of filling for the pyramid.

5 Peel off the baking paper from the large round of meringue, then place the filled meringues on top, piling them up in a pyramid. Keep them in position with a few well-placed dabs of the reserved filling. Dust the pyramid with icing sugar, sprinkle with the rose petals and serve immediately.

Nutritional information: Energy 701kcal/2941kJ; Protein 8.2g; Carbohydrate 94.2g, of which sugars 93.1g; Fat 35g, of which saturates 21g; Cholesterol 12mg; Calcium 49mg; Fibre 3g; Sodium 31mg.

Chocolate and orange angel cake

This light cake is very low in fat, but still looks impressive enough for a special occasion, as well as satisfying the most demanding sweet tooth.

SERVES 10

25g/1oz/¼ cup plain (all-purpose) flour
30ml/2 tbsp unsweetened cocoa powder
30ml/2 tbsp cornflour (cornstarch)
pinch of salt
5 egg whites
2.5ml/½ tsp cream of tartar
115g/4oz/½ cup caster (superfine)
   sugar
blanched and shredded rind of 1 orange,
   to decorate

FOR THE ICING

200g/7oz/scant 1 cup caster
   (superfine) sugar
75ml/5 tbsp cold water
1 egg white

1 Preheat the oven to 180°C/350°F/Gas 4. Sift the flour, cocoa, cornflour and salt together three times. Whisk the egg whites in a large bowl until foamy. Add the cream of tartar to the egg whites and whisk until soft peaks form.

2 Add the caster sugar to the egg whites a spoonful at a time, whisking after each addition. Add, by sifting, a third of the flour and cocoa mixture, and gently fold in. Repeat, sifting and folding in the flour and cocoa two more times. Spoon the mixture into a 20cm/8in non-stick ring tin (pan) and level the top. Bake for 35 minutes or until springy when lightly pressed. Turn upside down on to a wire rack and leave to cool in the tin.

3 For the icing, put the sugar in a pan with the water. Stir over a low heat until dissolved. Boil until the syrup reaches a temperature of 120°C/250°F on a sugar thermometer. Remove from the heat. Ease the cake out of the tin.

4 Whisk the egg white until stiff. Add the syrup in a thin stream, whisking all the time. Continue to whisk until the mixture is very thick and fluffy. Spread the icing over the top and sides of the cooled cake. Sprinkle the orange rind over the top of the cake.

Nutritional information: Energy 150kcal/637kJ; Protein 24.1g; Carbohydrate 364.1g, of which sugars 329.6g; Fat 3.7g, of which saturates 2g; Cholesterol 0mg; Calcium 233mg; Fibre 2.6g; Sodium 535mg.

Caribbean chocolate ring with rum syrup

Lavish and colourful, this exotic chocolate gateau can be made in advance, then, just before serving, add the syrup and fruit. It will add a touch of glamour to any table.

SERVES 8–10

115g/4oz/¹⁄₂ cup unsalted (sweet) butter
115g/4oz/³⁄₄ cup light muscovado
    (brown) sugar
2 eggs, beaten
2 ripe bananas, mashed
30ml/2 tbsp desiccated (dry
    unsweetened shredded) coconut
30ml/2 tbsp sour cream
115g/4oz/1 cup self-raising
    (self-rising) flour
2.5ml/¹⁄₂ tsp bicarbonate of soda
    (baking soda)
45ml/3 tbsp unsweetened cocoa powder
tropical fruits and chocolate curls,
    to decorate

FOR THE SYRUP

115g/4oz/¹⁄₂ cup caster (superfine) sugar
60ml/4 tbsp water
30ml/2 tbsp dark rum
50g/2oz dark (bittersweet)
    chocolate, chopped

1 Preheat the oven to 180°C/350°F/Gas 4. Grease a 1.5-litre/2¹⁄₂-pint/6¹⁄₄-cup ring tin (pan).

2 Place the butter and sugar in a large bowl. Cream together until light and fluffy. Beat in the eggs gradually, beating well, then mix in the bananas, coconut and cream. Sift the flour, bicarbonate of soda and cocoa over the mixture and fold in.

3 Turn the mixture into the prepared tin and spread evenly. Bake for 45–50 minutes until firm to the touch. Allow to cool for 10 minutes in the tin, then turn out to cool completely on a wire rack.

4 To make the syrup, heat the sugar and water gently in a pan until the sugar is completely dissolved. Bring to the boil and boil rapidly for 2 minutes. Remove from the heat.

5 Add the rum and chocolate and stir until melted and smooth, then spoon the syrup over the top of the cake. Decorate the ring with tropical fruits and chocolate curls.

Nutritional information: Energy 322kcal/1351kJ; Protein 4.1g; Carbohydrate 41.7g, of which sugars 31.9g; Fat 15.6g, of which saturates 9.7g; Cholesterol 65mg; Calcium 48mg; Fibre 1.7g; Sodium 131mg.

White chocolate mousse and strawberry layer cake

Make this spectacular cake in summer, when strawberries are at their best. It would be a wonderful choice for a special garden party.

SERVES 10

115g/4oz white chocolate, chopped into
    small pieces
120ml/4fl oz/^{1}/2 cup double
    (heavy) cream
120ml/4fl oz/^{1}/2 cup milk
15ml/1 tbsp rum or vanilla extract
115g/4oz/^{1}/2 cup unsalted (sweet)
    butter, softened
175g/6oz/^{3}/4 cup sugar
3 eggs
225g/8oz/2 cups plain (all-purpose) flour
10ml/2 tsp baking powder
pinch of salt

675g/1^1/2lb fresh strawberries, sliced,
    plus extra for decoration
750ml/1^1/4 pints/3 cups whipping cream
30ml/2 tbsp rum or strawberry liqueur

FOR THE WHITE CHOCOLATE MOUSSE FILLING

250g/9oz white chocolate, chopped into
    small pieces
350ml/12fl oz/1^1/2 cups double
    (heavy) cream
30ml/2 tbsp rum or strawberry liqueur

1 Preheat the oven to 180°C/350°F/Gas 4. Grease and flour two 23 x 5cm/ 9 x 2in cake tins (pans). Line the bases with baking parchment. Melt the chocolate and cream in a double boiler over a low heat, stirring until smooth. Stir in the milk and rum or vanilla extract, and set aside to cool.

2 In a large mixing bowl, beat the butter and sugar with a hand-held electric mixer for 3–5 minutes, until light and creamy, scraping the sides of the bowl occasionally. Add the eggs one at a time, beating well after each addition. In a small bowl, stir together the flour, baking powder and salt. Alternately add flour and melted chocolate to the egg mixture in batches, until just blended. Pour the mixture into the tins and spread evenly.

3 Bake for 20–25 minutes, until a skewer inserted in the cake comes out clean. Cool in the tin for 10 minutes, then turn the cakes out on to a wire rack, peel off the paper and cool completely.

4 Make the mousse filling. In a medium pan over a low heat, melt the chocolate and cream until smooth, stirring frequently. Stir in the rum or strawberry liqueur and pour into a bowl. Cool, then chill until just set. With a wire whisk, whip lightly.

5 With a serrated knife, slice both cake layers in half, making four layers. Place one layer on the plate and spread one-third of the mousse on top. Arrange one-third of the sliced strawberries over the mousse. Place the second layer on top and spread with another third of the mousse. Arrange another third of the strawberries over the mousse.

6 Place the third layer on top and spread with the remaining mousse. Cover with the remaining sliced strawberries. Top with the last cake layer. Whip the cream with the rum until firm peaks form. Spread the whipped cream over the top and sides of the cake. Decorate with the remaining sliced strawberries.

Nutritional information: Energy 1011kcal/4196kJ; Protein 10.3g; Carbohydrate 64.6g, of which sugars 47.4g; Fat 79g, of which saturates 48.3g; Cholesterol 227mg; Calcium 242mg; Fibre 1.4g; Sodium 171mg.

White chocolate cappuccino gateau

Luscious, lavish and laced with liqueur, this truly decadent combination of white chocolate and strong black coffee is strictly for adults only!

SERVES 8

4 eggs
115g/4oz/¹/₂ cup caster (superfine)
    sugar
15ml/1 tbsp strong black coffee
2.5ml/¹/₂ tsp vanilla extract
115g/4oz/1 cup plain (all-purpose) flour
75g/3oz white chocolate, coarsely grated

FOR THE FILLING
120ml/4fl oz/¹/₂ cup double (heavy) cream
15ml/1 tbsp coffee liqueur

FOR THE FROSTING AND TOPPING
15ml/1 tbsp coffee liqueur
1 quantity White Chocolate Frosting
white chocolate curls
unsweetened cocoa powder or ground
    cinnamon, for dusting

1 Preheat the oven to 180°C/350°F/Gas 4. Grease two 19cm/7¹/₂in round sandwich cake tins (pans) and line the base of each with baking parchment.

2 Combine the eggs, caster sugar, coffee and vanilla extract in a heatproof bowl. Place over a pan of simmering water and whisk until the mixture is pale and thick enough to hold its shape when the whisk is lifted.

3 Sift half the flour over the mixture; fold in gently and evenly. Fold in the remaining flour with the grated white chocolate. Divide the mixture between the prepared tins and smooth level. Bake for 20–25 minutes, until firm and golden brown, then turn out on wire racks and leave to cool completely.

4 For the filling, whip the cream with the liqueur in a bowl until it holds its shape. Spread over one of the cakes, then place the second layer on top.

5 Stir the coffee liqueur into the frosting. Spread over the top and sides of the cake, swirling with a metal spatula. Top with curls of white chocolate and dust with cocoa or cinnamon.

Nutritional information: Energy 337kcal/1418kJ; Protein 5.3g; Carbohydrate 50.5g, of which sugars 39.5g; Fat 13.6g, of which saturates 7.4g; Cholesterol 116mg; Calcium 61mg; Fibre 0.7g; Sodium 41mg.

French chocolate cake

The classic slim shape and simple design of this cake belies its unbelievably rich taste. The cake is turned upside down after baking, giving it a beautifully smooth surface.

SERVES 10

250g/9oz dark (bittersweet) chocolate, chopped into small pieces
225g/8oz/1 cup unsalted (sweet) butter, cut into small pieces
90g/3¹/₂oz/scant ¹/₂ cup sugar
30ml/2 tbsp brandy or orange-flavoured liqueur
5 eggs
15ml/1 tbsp plain (all-purpose) flour
icing (confectioners') sugar, for dusting
whipped or sour cream, for serving

1 Preheat the oven to 180°C/350°F/Gas 4. Grease a 23 x 5cm/9 x 2in springform tin (pan). Line the base with baking parchment and grease. Wrap the bottom and sides of the tin in foil to prevent water from seeping into the cake. Melt the chocolate, butter and sugar gently in a pan, stirring frequently until smooth. Remove from the heat, cool slightly and stir in the brandy or liqueur.

2 Beat the eggs for 1 minute. Beat in the flour, then slowly beat in the chocolate mixture until blended. Pour into the prepared tin. Place in a large roasting pan. Add enough boiling water to come 2cm/³/₄in up the side of the springform tin.

3 Bake for 30 minutes until the edge of the cake is set but the centre is still soft. Remove the springform tin from the roasting pan and remove the foil. Cool in the tin on a wire rack. The cake will sink in the centre. Don't worry if the surface cracks. Turn the cake on to a wire rack. Lift off the springform tin base and peel back the paper, so the base of the cake is now the top.

4 Cut 8 strips of baking parchment 2.5cm/1in wide and place randomly over the cake. Dust the cake with icing sugar, then remove the paper. Slide the cake on to a plate and serve with whipped or sour cream.

Nutritional information: Energy 380kcal/1586kJ; Protein 50.6g; Carbohydrate 363.5g, of which sugars 330.6g; Fat 249.1g, of which saturates 145.2g; Cholesterol 1341mg; Calcium 400mg; Fibre 8.1g; Sodium 1437mg.

Hazelnut and chocolate cake

This silky chocolate cake marries the satisfying crunch of hazelnuts with just a hint of sweet orange for a unusual but delicious treat.

SERVES 10

150g/5oz plain (semisweet) chocolate

115g/4oz/¹/₂ cup unsalted (sweet) butter, softened

115g/4oz/¹/₂ cup caster (superfine) sugar

4 eggs, separated

115g/4oz/1 cup ground lightly toasted hazelnuts

50g/2oz/1 cup fresh breadcrumbs

grated rind of 1¹/₂ oranges

30ml/2 tbsp sieved marmalade, warmed

60ml/4 tbsp chopped hazelnuts, to decorate

FOR THE ICING

150g/5oz plain (semisweet) chocolate, chopped into small pieces

50g/2oz/¹/₄ cup butter, diced

1 Preheat the oven to 180°C/350°F/Gas 4. Butter a 23cm/9in round cake tin (pan) and line the base with baking parchment.

2 Melt the chocolate and set aside. Beat the butter and sugar together, then gradually add the egg yolks, beating well. The mixture may curdle slightly. Beat in the melted chocolate, then the hazelnuts, breadcrumbs and orange rind. Whisk the egg whites until stiff, then fold into the chocolate mixture. Transfer to the cake tin. Bake for 40–45 minutes, until set.

3 Remove from the oven, cover with a damp dish towel for 5 minutes, then transfer to a wire rack until cold.

4 Make the icing. Place the chocolate and butter in a heatproof bowl over a pan of simmering water and stir until smooth. Leave until cool and thick. Spread the cake with the marmalade, then the icing. Sprinkle over the nuts, then leave to set.

Nutritional information: Energy 490kcal/2040kJ; Protein 7.2g; Carbohydrate 38.2g, of which sugars 33.8g; Fat 35.4g, of which saturates 15.1g; Cholesterol 113mg; Calcium 62mg; Fibre 2g; Sodium 172mg.

Vegan chocolate gateau

A divine dairy-free alternative that contains the goodness of wholemeal flour, this gateau is topped with a rich fudge frosting that will please everyone, vegan or not.

SERVES 8–10

275g/10oz/2¹/₂ cups self-raising wholemeal (self-rising whole-wheat) flour
50g/2oz/¹/₂ cup unsweetened cocoa powder
45ml/3 tbsp baking powder
225g/8oz/1¹/₄ cups caster (superfine) sugar
few drops of vanilla extract
135ml/9 tbsp sunflower oil
350ml/12fl oz/1¹/₂ cups water

sifted unsweetened cocoa powder, for dusting
25g/1oz/¹/₄ cup chopped nuts, to decorate

FOR THE CHOCOLATE FUDGE
50g/2oz/¹/₄ cup vegan (soya) margarine
45ml/3 tbsp water
250g/9oz/2 cups icing (confectioners') sugar, sifted
30ml/2 tbsp unsweetened cocoa powder, sifted
15–30ml/1–2 tbsp hot water

1 Preheat the oven to 160°C/325°F/Gas 3. Grease a 20cm/8in round cake tin (pan), line with baking parchment and grease the paper. Sift the flour, cocoa and baking powder into a bowl. Add the caster sugar and vanilla, then gradually beat in the oil. Add the water in the same way, beating to produce a smooth mixture the consistency of a thick batter. Pour into the prepared tin and level the surface.

2 Bake for 45 minutes, or until a skewer inserted in the centre comes out clean. Remove from the oven, leave in the tin for 5 minutes, then turn out on to a wire rack. Peel off the paper and leave to cool. Cut in half to make two layers.

3 For the chocolate fudge, heat the margarine and water gently until the margarine has melted. Remove from the heat and add the sifted icing sugar and cocoa powder, beating until shiny, adding more hot water if needed. Pour into a bowl and cool until firm enough to spread and pipe.

4 Place the bottom layer of the cake on a plate and spread over two-thirds of the chocolate fudge. Top with the other layer. Fit a piping bag with a star nozzle, fill with the remaining chocolate fudge and pipe stars over the cake. Sprinkle with cocoa powder and decorate with chopped nuts.

Nutritional information: Energy 442kcal/1862kJ; Protein 4.7g; Carbohydrate 74.7g, of which sugars 52.8g; Fat 15.9g, of which saturates 2.2g; Cholesterol 0mg; Calcium 78mg; Fibre 1.9g; Sodium 120mg.

Rich chocolate leaf gateau

Thick, creamy chocolate ganache and chocolate leaves decorate this mouthwatering gateau. Serve with creamy coffee or tea for an indulgent afternoon snack.

SERVES 12–14

150ml/¼ pint/²/₃ cup milk

75g/3oz dark (bittersweet) chocolate, broken into squares

175g/6oz/¾ cup unsalted (sweet) butter, softened

250g/9oz/1½ cups light muscovado (brown) sugar

3 eggs

250g/9oz/2¼ cups plain (all-purpose) flour

10ml/2 tsp baking powder

75ml/5 tbsp single (light) cream

FOR THE FILLING AND TOPPING

60ml/4 tbsp raspberry conserve

1 quantity Chocolate Ganache

dark and white chocolate leaves

1 Preheat the oven to 190°C/375°F/ Gas 5. Grease two 22cm/8½in sandwich cake tins (pans) and line the base of each with baking parchment. Stir the milk and chocolate in a pan over a low heat until smooth. Allow to cool slightly.

2 Cream the butter with the sugar in a bowl until pale and fluffy. Beat in the eggs one at a time, beating well after each addition.

3 Sift the flour and baking powder over the mixture and fold in. Stir in the melted chocolate mixture with the cream, mixing until smooth.

4 Divide between the prepared tins and level the tops. Bake for 30–35 minutes or until the cakes are well risen and firm to the touch. Allow the cakes to cool in the tins for a few minutes, then carefully turn out on to wire racks and leave until cold.

5 Sandwich the cake layers together with the raspberry conserve.

6 Spread the chocolate ganache over the top and sides of the cake. Swirl the ganache with a knife. Place the cake on a serving plate, then decorate with the dark and white chocolate leaves.

Nutritional information: Energy 476kcal/1986kJ; Protein 5.3g; Carbohydrate 49.4g, of which sugars 35.7g; Fat 29.9g, of which saturates 18.2g; Cholesterol 102mg; Calcium 84mg; Fibre 1g; Sodium 108mg.

Strawberry chocolate valentine gateau

Offering a slice of this voluptuous valentine gateau could be the start of a very special romance. Don't forget the chocolate hearts, for that extra special touch.

SERVES 8

175g/6oz/1½ cups self-raising (self-
   rising) flour
10ml/2 tsp baking powder
75ml/5 tbsp unsweetened cocoa powder
115g/4oz/½ cup caster (superfine) sugar
2 eggs, beaten
15ml/1 tbsp black treacle (molasses)
150ml/¼ pint/⅔ cup sunflower oil
150ml/¼ pint/⅔ cup milk

FOR THE FILLING

45ml/3 tbsp strawberry jam
150ml/¼ pint/⅔ cup double (heavy) or
   whipping cream
115g/4oz strawberries, sliced

TO DECORATE

1 quantity Chocolate Fondant
chocolate hearts
icing (confectioners') sugar,
   for dusting

1 Preheat the oven to 160°C/325°F/ Gas 3. Grease a deep 20cm/8in heart-shaped cake tin (pan) and line the base with baking parchment.

2 Sift the flour, baking powder and cocoa into a bowl. Stir in the sugar. Make a well in the centre and add the eggs, treacle, oil and milk. Mix to incorporate the dry ingredients, then beat with a hand-held electric mixer until smooth and creamy. Spoon the mixture into the prepared tin. Bake for 45 minutes or until risen and firm to the touch.

3 Cool the cake in the tin for a few minutes, then turn out on to a wire rack to cool completely. Slice the cake into two layers, and spread the bottom layer with the jam.

4 Whip the cream until it holds its shape. Stir in the strawberries, then spread over the jam. Top with the remaining cake layer.

5 Roll out the chocolate fondant and cover the cake. Decorate with chocolate hearts and dust with icing sugar.

Nutritional information: Energy 395kcal/1649kJ; Protein 6.5g; Carbohydrate 40.2g, of which sugars 22.5g; Fat 24.3g, of which saturates 8.1g; Cholesterol 68mg; Calcium 100mg; Fibre 2g; Sodium 126mg.

Chocolate and beetroot layer cake

Beetroot and chocolate might seem a surprising combination, but the beetroot in this cake adds a subtle sweetness that really enhances the chocolate flavour.

SERVES 10–12

unsweetened cocoa powder, for dusting

225g/8oz can cooked whole beetroot, drained and juice reserved

115g/4oz/1/2 cup unsalted (sweet) butter, softened

425g/15oz/21/2 cups soft light brown sugar

3 eggs

15ml/1 tbsp vanilla extract

75g/3oz dark (bittersweet) chocolate, melted

225g/8oz/2 cups plain (all-purpose) flour

10ml/2 tsp baking powder

2.5ml/1/2 tsp salt

120ml/4fl oz/1/2 cup buttermilk

chocolate curls (optional)

CHOCOLATE GANACHE FROSTING

475ml/16fl oz/2 cups whipping cream or double (heavy) cream

500g/11/4lb dark (bittersweet) or plain (semisweet) chocolate, chopped into small pieces

15ml/1 tbsp vanilla extract

1 Preheat the oven to 180°C/350°F/Gas 4. Grease two 23cm/9in cake tins (pans) and dust the base and sides with cocoa. Grate the beetroot and add to the juice. Set aside. With a hand-held electric mixer, beat the butter, brown sugar, eggs and vanilla extract in a bowl until pale. Reduce the speed and beat in the melted chocolate. Sift the flour, baking powder and salt into a separate bowl.

2 With the mixer on low speed, gradually beat the flour mixture into the butter mixture, alternately with the buttermilk. Add the beetroot and juice and beat for 1 minute. Divide between the tins and bake for 30–35 minutes or until a cake tester inserted in the centre of each cake comes out clean. Cool in the tins for 10 minutes, then turn the cakes out on a wire rack and cool completely.

3 For the ganache frosting, heat the cream in a pan over medium heat, until it just begins to boil, stirring occasionally to prevent it scorching. Remove from the heat and stir in the chocolate, stirring constantly until melted and smooth. Stir in the vanilla extract. Strain into a bowl. Cool, then chill, stirring every 10 minutes for about 1 hour, until spreadable.

4 Assemble the cake. Place one layer on a serving plate and spread with one-third of the frosting. Place the second layer on top and spread the remaining frosting over the cake and down the sides. Decorate with chocolate curls, if using. Leave to set for 20–30 minutes, then chill before serving.

Nutritional information: Energy 699kcal/2925kJ; Protein 7.4g; Carbohydrate 85.1g, of which sugars 70.3g; Fat 38.9g, of which saturates 23.5g; Cholesterol 113mg; Calcium 109mg; Fibre 2.1g; Sodium 108mg.

Death by chocolate

*This is one of the richest chocolate cakes ever, and so should be served in very thin slices.
True chocoholics can always come back for second helpings!*

SERVES 16–20

225g/8oz dark (bittersweet) chocolate,
   chopped into squares
115g/4oz/1/2 cup unsalted (sweet) butter
150ml/1/4 pint/2/3 cup milk
225g/8oz/11/4 cups soft light brown sugar
10ml/2 tsp vanilla extract
2 eggs, separated
150ml/1/4 pint/2/3 cup sour cream
225g/8oz/2 cups self-raising
   (self-rising) flour
5ml/1 tsp baking powder

FOR THE FILLING AND TOPPING
60ml/4 tbsp seedless raspberry jam
60ml/4 tbsp brandy
400g/14oz dark (bittersweet) chocolate
200g/7oz/scant 1 cup unsalted
   (sweet) butter
1 quantity Chocolate Ganache , plain
   (semisweet), milk and white Chocolate
   Curls, to decorate

1 Preheat the oven to 180°C/350°F/Gas 4. Grease and base-line a 23cm/9in springform cake tin (pan). Gently heat the chocolate, butter and milk in a pan, stirring until smooth. Remove from the heat, beat in the sugar and vanilla, then cool.

2 Beat the egg yolks and cream, then beat into the chocolate mix. Sift the flour and baking powder over and fold in. Whisk the egg whites until stiff; fold into the mixture. Spoon into the tin and bake for 45–55 minutes until firm to the touch. Cool in the tin for 15 minutes, then turn out on to a wire rack to cool completely in the tin.

3 Slice the cake into three layers. Warm the jam with 15ml/1 tbsp of the brandy, then brush over two layers and leave to set. Heat the chocolate in a pan with the remaining brandy and butter, stirring, until smooth. Cool slightly.

4 Spread the bottom layer of the cake with half the filling. Top with a second layer, jam side up, and spread with the remaining filling. Top with the final layer. Leave to set, then cover with ganache. Decorate with chocolate curls.

Nutritional information: Energy 432kcal/1809kJ; Protein 4.7g; Carbohydrate 49.9g, of which sugars 38.4g; Fat 24.7g, of which saturates 14.9g; Cholesterol 57mg; Calcium 99mg; Fibre 1.4g; Sodium 120mg.

Chocolate and cherry polenta cake

Perfect for packing to take on a romantic picnic, this chocolate cherry cake is dense and delicious. Polenta and almonds add a moist richness to the texture.

SERVES 8

50g/2oz/¹⁄₃ cup quick-cook polenta
200g/7oz plain (semisweet) chocolate,
    broken into squares
5 eggs, separated
175g/6oz /³⁄₄ cup caster (superfine)
    sugar
115g/4oz/1 cup ground almonds
60ml/4 tbsp plain (all-purpose) flour
finely grated rind of 1 orange
115g/4oz/¹⁄₂ cup glacé (candied)
    cherries, halved
icing (confectioners') sugar, for dusting

1 Place the polenta in a heatproof bowl and pour over enough boiling water to cover; about 120ml/4fl oz/¹⁄₂ cup. Stir well, cover the bowl and leave to stand for 30 minutes, until the polenta has absorbed all of the excess moisture.

2 Preheat the oven to 190°C/375°F/Gas 5. Grease a deep 22cm/8¹⁄₂in round cake tin (pan) and line the base with baking parchment. Melt the chocolate gently in a heatproof bowl set over a pan of simmering water.

3 Whisk the egg yolks with the sugar in a bowl until thick and pale. Beat in the chocolate, then fold in the polenta, ground almonds, flour and orange rind.

4 Whisk the egg whites in a clean, grease-free bowl until stiff. Stir 15ml/ 1 tbsp of the whites into the chocolate mixture to lighten it, then fold in the rest. Finally, fold in the cherries. Spoon the mixture into the tin and bake for 45–55 minutes until well risen and firm to the touch. Turn out and cool on a wire rack, then dust with icing sugar to serve.

Nutritional information: Energy 420kcal/1764kJ; Protein 9.6g; Carbohydrate 56.4g, of which sugars 45.5g; Fat 18.8g, of which saturates 5.8g; Cholesterol 120mg; Calcium 89mg; Fibre 2.2g; Sodium 53mg.

Black Forest gateau

This luscious chocolate sponge, moistened with Kirsch and layered with cherries and cream, is still one of the most popular chocolate gateaux.

SERVES 8–10

6 eggs
200g/7oz/scant 1 cup caster (superfine)
    sugar
5ml/1 tsp vanilla extract
50g/2oz/¹/₂ cup plain (all-purpose) flour
50g/2oz/¹/₂ cup unsweetened cocoa
    powder
115g/4oz/¹/₂ cup unsalted (sweet)
    butter, melted
60ml/4 tbsp Kirsch

FOR THE FILLING AND TOPPING
600ml/1 pint/2¹/₂ cups double
    (heavy) cream
30ml/2 tbsp icing (confectioners') sugar
2.5ml/¹/₂ tsp vanilla extract
675g/1¹/₂lb jar pitted morello cherries
Grated Chocolate
Chocolate Curls
fresh or drained canned morello cherries

1 Preheat the oven to 180°C/350°F/Gas 4. Grease three 19cm/7¹/₂in sandwich cake tins (pans) and line the bases with baking parchment. Whisk the eggs with the sugar and vanilla in a bowl until pale and very thick. Sift the flour and cocoa over the mixture and fold in. Stir in the melted butter.

2 Divide the mixture among the tins, smoothing them level. Bake for 15–18 minutes until risen and springy to the touch. Cool in the tins for 5 minutes, then turn out on to wire racks and leave to cool completely.

3 Prick each layer with a skewer, then sprinkle with Kirsch. Whip the cream until it starts to thicken, then beat in the icing sugar and vanilla until the mixture holds its shape. Spread a cake layer with a quarter of the cream and top with a quarter of the cherries. Spread a second cake layer with cream and cherries, then place it on top of the first. Top with the final layer.

4 Spread the remaining cream all over the cake. Press grated chocolate over the sides and decorate with the chocolate curls and cherries.

Nutritional information: Energy 570kcal/2371kJ; Protein 2.9g; Carbohydrate 44g, of which sugars 39.6g; Fat 42.8g, of which saturates 26.7g; Cholesterol 107mg; Calcium 67mg; Fibre 1.2g; Sodium 137mg.

Simple chocolate cake

An easy, everyday chocolate cake that can be simply filled with buttercream, or pepped up with a rich chocolate ganache for a special occasion.

SERVES 6–8

115g/4oz plain (semisweet) chocolate, broken into squares

45ml/3 tbsp milk

150g/5oz/²/₃ cup unsalted (sweet) butter or margarine, softened

150g/5oz/scant 1 cup light muscovado (brown) sugar

3 eggs

200g/7oz/1³/₄ cups self-raising (self-rising) flour

15ml/1 tbsp unsweetened cocoa powder

1 quantity Chocolate Buttercream

icing (confectioners') sugar and cocoa powder, for dusting

1 Preheat the oven to 180°C/350°F/Gas 4. Grease two 18cm/7in round sandwich cake tins (pans) and line the base of each with baking parchment. Melt the chocolate with the milk in a heatproof bowl set over a pan of simmering water.

2 Cream the butter or margarine with the sugar in a mixing bowl until pale and fluffy. Add the eggs one at a time, beating well after each addition. Stir in the chocolate mixture until well combined.

3 Sift the flour and cocoa over the mixture and fold in with a metal spoon until evenly mixed. Scrape into the prepared tins, smooth level and bake for 35–40 minutes or until well risen and firm. Turn out on to wire racks to cool completely. Sandwich the cake layers together with the buttercream. Dust with a mixture of icing sugar and cocoa just before serving.

Nutritional information: Energy 427kcal/1776kJ; Protein 6.1g; Carbohydrate 29.2g, of which sugars 9.8g; Fat 32.6g, of which saturates 19.6g; Cholesterol 139mg; Calcium 65mg; Fibre 1.4g; Sodium 238mg.

One-mix chocolate sponge

This ridiculously easy-to-make chocolate cake, with its marmalade and cream filling, produces great results, time after time, with the smallest amount of effort.

SERVES 8–10

175g/6oz/³/4 cup soft margarine, at room
   temperature
115g/4oz/¹/2 cup caster (superfine)
   sugar
60ml/4 tbsp golden (light corn) syrup
175g/6oz/1¹/2 cups self-raising (self-
   rising) flour, sifted
30ml/2 tbsp unsweetened cocoa
   powder, sifted
2.5ml/¹/2 tsp salt
3 eggs, beaten
little milk (optional)
150ml/¹/4 pint/²/3 cup whipping cream
15–30ml/1–2 tbsp finely
   shredded marmalade
sifted icing (confectioners') sugar, to
   decorate

1 Preheat the oven to 180°C/350°F/Gas 4. Grease two 18cm/7in sandwich cake tins (pans). Cream the margarine, sugar, syrup, flour, cocoa, salt and eggs in a large bowl.

2 If the mixture seems a little thick, stir in enough milk to give a soft dropping (pourable) consistency. Spoon the mixture into the prepared tins, and bake for about 30 minutes, changing shelves if necessary after 15 minutes, until just firm and springy to the touch.

3 Leave the cakes to cool in the tins for 5 minutes, then remove from the tins and leave to cool completely on a wire rack.

4 Whip the cream and fold in the marmalade. Use the mixture to sandwich the two cakes together. Sprinkle the top with sifted icing sugar.

Nutritional information: Energy 162kcal/675kJ; Protein 13.1g; Carbohydrate 8.5g, of which sugars 7g; Fat 8.6g, of which saturates 3.8g; Cholesterol 44mg; Calcium 42mg; Fibre 3g; Sodium 55mg.

Marbled Swiss roll

Simply sensational – that's the combination of light chocolate sponge and walnut chocolate buttercream in this twist on a popular recipe.

SERVES 6–8

90g/3¹/₂oz/scant 1 cup plain (all-purpose) flour

15ml/1 tbsp unsweetened cocoa powder

25g/1oz plain (semisweet) chocolate, grated

25g/1oz white chocolate, grated

3 eggs

115g/4oz/¹/₂ cup caster (superfine) sugar

30ml/2 tbsp boiling water

plain (semisweet) and white chocolate curls, to decorate

FOR THE FILLING

1 quantity Chocolate Buttercream

45ml/3 tbsp chopped walnuts

1 Preheat the oven to 200°C/400°F/Gas 6. Grease a 30 x 20cm/12 x 8in Swiss roll tin (jelly roll pan) and line with baking parchment. Sift half the flour with the cocoa into a bowl. Stir in the grated plain chocolate. Sift the remaining flour into another bowl; stir in the grated white chocolate.

2 Whisk the eggs and sugar in a heatproof bowl set over a pan of simmering water until the mixture holds its shape when the whisk is lifted. Remove from the heat and put half the mixture into a separate bowl. Fold the white chocolate mixture into one portion, then fold the plain chocolate mixture into the other. Stir 15ml/1 tbsp boiling water into each half to soften.

3 Place alternate spoonfuls of mixture in the prepared tin and swirl for a marbled effect. Bake for 15 minutes, or until firm. Turn on to a sheet of baking parchment. Trim the edges and cover with a damp, clean dish towel. Cool.

4 For the filling, mix the buttercream and walnuts in a bowl. Uncover the sponge, lift off the paper and spread the surface with the buttercream. Roll up from a long side and place on a plate. Decorate with chocolate curls.

Nutritional information: Energy 361kcal/1518kJ; Protein 5.6g; Carbohydrate 51.1g, of which sugars 42g; Fat 16.4g, of which saturates 7.4g; Cholesterol 92mg; Calcium 67mg; Fibre 1.1g; Sodium 125mg.

Chocolate roulade

If you can't get a block of creamed coconut, you could use desiccated (dry unsweetened shredded) coconut for the filling instead – it will still be rich and delicious.

SERVES 8

150g/5oz/³⁄₄ cup caster (superfine) sugar
5 eggs, separated
50g/2oz/¹⁄₂ cup unsweetened cocoa powder

FOR THE FILLING
300ml/¹⁄₂ pint/1¹⁄₄ cups double (heavy) cream
45ml/3 tbsp whisky

50g/2oz piece solid creamed coconut
30ml/2 tbsp caster (superfine) sugar

FOR THE TOPPING
coarsely grated curls of fresh coconut
chocolate curls

1 Preheat the oven to 180°C/350°C/Gas 4. Grease a 32 x 23cm/13 x 9in Swiss roll tin (jelly roll pan) and line with baking parchment. Dust a large sheet of baking parchment with 30ml/2 tbsp of the sugar.

2 Place the egg yolks in a heatproof bowl. Add the remaining sugar and whisk with a hand-held electric mixer until the mixture is thick enough to leave a trail. Sift the cocoa over, then fold in carefully and evenly with a metal spoon.

3 Whisk the egg whites in a clean, grease-free bowl until they form soft peaks. Fold about 15ml/1 tbsp of the whites into the chocolate mixture to lighten it, then fold in the rest evenly.

4 Scrape the mixture into the prepared tin, taking it right into the corners. Smooth the surface with a metal spatula, then bake for 20–25 minutes or until well risen and springy to the touch.

5 Turn the cooked roulade out on to the sugar-dusted baking parchment and carefully peel off the lining paper. Cover with a damp, clean dish towel and leave to cool.

6 Make the filling. Whisk the cream with the whisky in a bowl until the mixture just holds its shape, then finely grate the creamed coconut and stir it in with the sugar.

7 Uncover the sponge and spread about three-quarters of the cream mixture to the edges. Roll up carefully from a long side. Transfer to a plate, pipe or spoon the remaining cream mixture on top, then place the coconut curls on top with the chocolate curls.

Nutritional information: Energy 394kcal/1640kJ; Protein 6.2g; Carbohydrate 25.3g, of which sugars 24.6g; Fat 29.3g, of which saturates 18g; Cholesterol 170mg; Calcium 58mg; Fibre 0.8g; Sodium 115mg.

Chocolate chestnut roulade

This rich coffee-flavoured cake filled with delicious chestnut cream contains delicate hints of vanilla and rum for that decadent touch.

SERVES 10–12

175g/6oz dark (bittersweet) chocolate, chopped into small pieces
30ml/2 tbsp unsweetened cocoa powder, sifted
60ml/4 tbsp hot strong coffee or espresso
6 eggs, separated
75g/3oz/6 tbsp caster (superfine) sugar
pinch of cream of tartar
5ml/1 tsp vanilla extract
unsweetened cocoa powder, for dusting
glacé (candied) chestnuts, to decorate

FOR THE CHESTNUT CREAM FILLING
475ml/16fl oz/2 cups double (heavy) cream
30ml/2 tbsp rum or coffee-flavoured liqueur
350g/12oz/1^{1}/$_{2}$ cups canned sweetened chestnut purée
115g/4oz dark (bittersweet) chocolate, grated

1 Preheat the oven to 180°C/350°F/Gas 4. Lightly grease the base and sides of a 39 x 27 x 2.5cm/15^{1}/$_{2}$ x 10^{1}/$_{2}$ x 1in Swiss roll tin (jelly roll pan). Line with baking parchment, allowing a 2.5cm/1in overhang.

2 Melt the chocolate in a heatproof bowl set over a pan of simmering water. Blend the cocoa with the hot coffee to make a paste. Set aside.

3 Using a hand-held electric mixer, beat the egg yolks with half the sugar in a large bowl until pale and thick. Slowly beat in the melted chocolate and cocoa-coffee paste until just blended.

4 In a separate bowl, beat the egg whites and cream of tartar until stiff peaks form. Sprinkle the remaining sugar over the whites in two batches and beat until the whites are stiff and glossy, then beat in the vanilla extract.

5 Stir a spoonful of the whites into the chocolate mixture to lighten it, then fold in the rest. Spoon into the tin. Bake for 20–25 minutes or until the cake springs back when touched with a fingertip.

6 Dust a clean dish towel with cocoa. Turn the cake out on to the towel immediately and remove the paper. Trim off any crisp edges. Starting at a narrow end, roll the cake and towel together, Swiss roll fashion. Cool completely.

7 For the filling, whip the cream and rum or liqueur until soft peaks form. Beat a spoonful of cream into the chestnut purée, then fold in the remaining cream and grated chocolate. Set aside a quarter of this mixture for the decoration. Unroll the cake and spread chestnut cream to within 2.5cm/1in of the edge. Using a dish towel to lift the cake, carefully roll it up again. Place seam-side down on a serving plate. Spread some of the reserved chestnut cream over the top and use the rest for piped rosettes. Decorate with the glacé chestnuts.

Nutritional information: Energy 469kcal/1961kJ; Protein 6.2g; Carbohydrate 53.5g, of which sugars 44.9g; Fat 27.1g, of which saturates 15.2g; Cholesterol 163mg; Calcium 68mg; Fibre 1.7g; Sodium 57mg.

Sticky chocolate, maple and walnut swirls

This rich yeasted cake breaks into separate sticky chocolate swirls, each soaked in maple syrup. A sprinkle of walnuts gives them a crunchy texture.

SERVES 12

450g/1lb/4 cups strong white
    bread flour
2.5ml/1/2 tsp ground cinnamon
50g/2oz/4 tbsp unsalted (sweet) butter
50g/2oz/1/4 cup caster (superfine) sugar
1 sachet easy-blend (rapid-rise)
    dried yeast
1 egg yolk
120ml/4fl oz/1/2 cup water
60ml/4 tbsp milk
45ml/3 tbsp maple syrup

FOR THE FILLING

40g/11/2oz/3 tbsp unsalted (sweet)
    butter, melted
50g/2oz/1/3 cup light muscovado
    (brown) sugar
175g/6oz/1 cup plain (semisweet)
    chocolate chips
75g/3oz/3/4 cup chopped
    walnuts

1 Grease a deep 23cm/9in springform cake tin (pan). Sift the flour and cinnamon into a bowl, then rub in the butter until the mixture resembles coarse breadcrumbs. Stir in the sugar and yeast. Beat the egg yolk with the water and milk in a jug (pitcher), then stir into the dry ingredients to make a soft dough.

2 Knead the dough on a lightly floured surface until smooth, then roll out to a rectangle measuring about 40 x 30cm/16 x 12in. For the filling, brush the dough with the butter and sprinkle with the sugar, chocolate chips and nuts.

3 Roll up the dough from one long side like a Swiss (jelly) roll, then cut into 12 thick, even-size slices. Pack the slices closely together in the prepared tin, with the cut sides facing upwards. Cover and leave in a warm place for 11/2 hours, until well risen and springy to the touch. Meanwhile, preheat the oven to 220°C/425°F/Gas 7.

4 Bake for 30–35 minutes until well risen, golden brown and firm. Turn out on to a wire rack, brush or spoon maple syrup over the cake, then leave to cool. Pull the pieces apart to serve.

Nutritional information: Energy 418kcal/1747kJ; Protein 11.5g; Carbohydrate 51.8g, of which sugars 19.4g; Fat 15.9g, of which saturates 8.2g; Cholesterol 33mg; Calcium 209mg; Fibre 5.3g; Sodium 1195mg.

Chocolate chip walnut loaf

Perfect for that afternoon break with a cup of tea or coffee, this sweet and nutty loaf also includes a smattering of juicy currants.

MAKES 1 LOAF

115g/4oz/¹/2 cup caster
   (superfine) sugar
115g/4oz/1 cup plain
   (all-purpose) flour
5ml/1 tsp baking powder
60ml/4 tbsp cornflour (cornstarch)
115g/4 oz/¹/2 cup butter, softened
2 eggs, beaten
5ml/1 tsp vanilla extract
30ml/2 tbsp currants or raisins
25g/1oz/¹/4 cup walnuts, finely chopped
grated rind of ¹/2 lemon
45ml/3 tbsp plain (semisweet)
   chocolate chips
icing (confectioners') sugar, for dusting

1 Preheat the oven to 180°C/350°F/ Gas 4. Grease and line a 22 x 12cm/ 8¹/2 x 4¹/2in loaf tin (pan). Sprinkle 25ml/1¹/2 tbsp of the caster sugar into the tin in an even layer over the bottom and sides. Shake out excess sugar.

2 Sift the flour, baking powder and cornflour into a bowl. Repeat this twice more. Set aside. Using an electric mixer, cream the butter until soft. Add the remaining sugar and continue beating until light and fluffy. Add the eggs, one at a time, beating after each addition.

3 Gently fold the dry ingredients into the butter mixture, in three batches; do not overmix. Fold in the vanilla extract, currants or raisins, walnuts, lemon rind and chocolate chips, until just blended.

4 Pour the mixture into the prepared tin and bake for 45–50 minutes, until a skewer inserted in the centre comes out clean. Cool in the tin for 5 minutes before transferring to a rack to cool completely. Place on a serving plate and dust over an even layer of icing sugar before serving.

Nutritional information: Energy 3759kcal/15650kJ; Protein 60.1g; Carbohydrate 294g, of which sugars 149.5g; Fat 268.6g, of which saturates 76.5g; Cholesterol 626mg; Calcium 543mg; Fibre 12.5g; Sodium 913mg.

Bitter marmalade chocolate loaf

Don't be alarmed at the amount of cream in this recipe – it's naughty but necessary, and replaces butter to make a moist dark cake, topped with a bittersweet sticky marmalade glaze.

SERVES 8

115g/4oz plain (semisweet) chocolate, broken into squares

3 eggs

200g/7oz/scant 1 cup caster (superfine) sugar

175ml/6fl oz/¾ cup sour cream

200g/7oz/1¾ cups self-raising (self-rising) flour

FOR THE FILLING AND GLAZE

175g/6oz/⅔ cup bitter orange marmalade

115g/4oz plain (semisweet) chocolate, broken into squares

60ml/4 tbsp sour cream

shredded orange rind, to decorate

1 Preheat the oven to 180°C/350°F/Gas 4. Grease a 900g/2lb loaf tin (pan), then line it with baking parchment. Melt the chocolate in a heatproof bowl set over a pan of simmering water.

2 Combine the eggs and sugar in a bowl. Whisk the mixture until it is thick and creamy, then stir in the sour cream and chocolate. Fold in the flour. Spoon into the tin and bake for 1 hour until well risen and firm to the touch. Cool for a few minutes, then turn out on to a wire rack and cool completely.

3 Spoon two-thirds of the marmalade into a pan and melt over a low heat. Melt the chocolate and stir it into the marmalade with the sour cream.

4 Slice the cake across into three layers and sandwich together with half the marmalade filling. Spread the rest over the top of the cake and leave to set. Spoon the remaining marmalade over the cake and sprinkle with orange rind.

Nutritional information: Energy 475kcal/2004kJ; Protein 7.1g; Carbohydrate 80.1g, of which sugars 60.8g; Fat 16.3g, of which saturates 9.1g; Cholesterol 91mg; Calcium 101mg; Fibre 1.6g; Sodium 56mg.

Chocolate chip marzipan loaf

This rich loaf uses marzipan in an unusual way: chunks of it are mixed into the cake, along with chocolate chips, to make a fabulous taste combination.

MAKES 1 LOAF

115g/4oz/¹/₂ cup unsalted (sweet) butter, softened

150g/5oz/scant 1 cup light muscovado (brown) sugar

2 eggs, beaten

45ml/3 tbsp unsweetened cocoa powder

150g/5oz/1¹/₄ cups self-raising (self-rising) flour

130g/3¹/₂oz marzipan

60ml/4 tbsp plain (semisweet) chocolate chips

1 Preheat the oven to 180°C/350°F/Gas 4. Grease a 900g/2lb loaf tin (pan) and line the base with baking parchment. Cream the butter and sugar in a bowl until light and fluffy.

2 Add the eggs to the mixture one at a time, beating well after each addition to combine. Sift the cocoa and flour over the mixture and fold in evenly.

3 Chop the marzipan into small pieces with a sharp knife. Put the marzipan pieces into a bowl and mix with the chocolate chips. Set aside 60ml/4 tbsp and fold the rest evenly into the cake mixture.

4 Transfer into the prepared tin, level the top and sprinkle with the reserved marzipan and chocolate chips. Bake for 45 minutes or until the loaf is risen and firm. Cool slightly in the tin, then turn out on to a wire rack to cool completely.

Nutritional information: Energy 2919kcal/12240kJ; Protein 46.1g; Carbohydrate 368.6g, of which sugars 248.6g; Fat 150.7g, of which saturates 80.5g; Cholesterol 629mg; Calcium 513mg; Fibre 14.1g; Sodium 1305mg.

Hot desserts

Hot chocolate desserts appeal to anyone

who craves comforting food – the sweet

smell of warm chocolate from a Peachy

Chocolate Bake as it cooks is hard to

resist. If you're looking for something a

little special for a dinner party, offer

luscious poached pears swathed in

Chocolate Fudge Blankets.

Hot chocolate zabaglione

Once you've tasted this slinky, sensuous dessert, you'll never look at cocoa in quite the same way again. Serve in tall glasses to add glamour to any occasion.

SERVES 6

6 egg yolks
150g/5oz/²/₃ cup caster
    (superfine) sugar
45ml/3 tbsp unsweetened cocoa powder
200ml/7fl oz/scant 1 cup Marsala
cocoa powder or icing (confectioners')
    sugar, for dusting
chocolate cinnamon tuiles or amaretti,
    to serve (optional)

1 Half-fill a medium pan with water and bring to simmering point.

2 Select a heatproof bowl which will fit over the pan, place the egg yolks and sugar in it, and whisk until the mixture is pale and all the sugar has dissolved.

3 Add the cocoa powder and Marsala, then place the bowl over the simmering water.

4 Using a hand-held electric mixer, whisk the mixture until it is smooth, thick and foamy.

5 Pour the mixture quickly into tall heatproof glasses and dust lightly with cocoa powder or icing sugar.

6 Serve the zabaglione immediately, with a couple of chocolate cinnamon tuiles or amaretti biscuits, if you like.

Nutritional information: Energy 235kcal/989kJ; Protein 4.5g; Carbohydrate 31g, of which sugars 30.1g; Fat 7.1g, of which saturates 2.5g; Cholesterol 202mg; Calcium 48mg; Fibre 0.9g; Sodium 83mg.

Chocolate crêpes with plums and port

A good dinner party dessert, these fruit-filled crêpes are best served straight away, but you can save time by preparing the batter, filling and sauce in advance.

SERVES 6

50g/2oz plain (semisweet) chocolate,
    broken into squares
200ml/7fl oz/scant 1 cup milk
120ml/4fl oz/½ cup single (light) cream
30ml/2 tbsp unsweetened cocoa powder
115g/4oz/1 cup plain (all-purpose) flour
2 eggs
oil, for frying

FOR THE FILLING

500g/1¼ lb plums, halved and
    stoned (pitted)
50g/2oz/¼ cup caster (superfine) sugar
30ml/2 tbsp water
30ml/2 tbsp port
175g/6oz/¾ cup crème fraîche

FOR THE SAUCE

150g/5oz plain (semisweet) chocolate,
    broken into squares
175ml/6fl oz/¾ cup double (heavy) cream
15ml/1 tbsp port

1 Heat the chocolate and milk gently in a pan until the chocolate has melted. Pour into a blender or food processor and add the cream, cocoa powder, flour and eggs. Process until smooth, then pour into a jug (pitcher) and chill for 30 minutes.

2 Meanwhile, make the filling. Place the plums in a pan and add the sugar and water. Bring to the boil, then lower the heat, cover, and simmer for 10 minutes, until the plums are tender.

3 Stir the port into the plums and simmer for 30 seconds. Remove from the heat and keep warm.

4 Have ready a sheet of baking parchment. Heat a crêpe pan, add a little oil, then pour in just enough batter to evenly cover the base of the pan. Cook until the crêpe has set, then flip over to cook the other side. Slide on to the parchment, then cook 11 more crêpes in the same way.

5 For the sauce, combine the chocolate and cream in a pan. Heat gently, stirring until smooth. Add the port and heat, stirring, for 1 minute.

6 Divide the plum filling between the crêpes, add crème fraîche to each and roll up carefully. Serve with the sauce spooned over the top.

Nutritional information: Energy 867kcal/3604kJ; Protein 10.6g; Carbohydrate 57.4g, of which sugars 41.7g; Fat 67g, of which saturates 36.7g; Cholesterol 184mg; Calcium 175mg; Fibre 3.4g; Sodium 115mg.

Chocolate and orange Scotch pancakes

Served with a rich, creamy orange liqueur sauce, these Scotch pancakes are definitely more exciting than the traditional kind that are simply spread with butter.

SERVES 4

115g/4oz/1 cup self-raising
   (self-rising) flour
30ml/2 tbsp unsweetened cocoa powder
2 eggs
50g/2oz plain (semisweet) chocolate,
   broken into squares
200ml/7fl oz/scant 1 cup milk
finely grated rind of 1 orange
30ml/2 tbsp orange juice
butter or oil, for frying
60ml/4 tbsp chocolate curls,
   for sprinkling

FOR THE SAUCE

2 large oranges
30ml/2 tbsp unsalted (sweet) butter
45ml/3 tbsp light muscovado
   (brown) sugar
250ml/8fl oz/1 cup crème fraîche
30ml/2 tbsp Grand Marnier or Cointreau

1 Sift the flour and cocoa into a bowl and make a well in the centre. Add the eggs and beat well, incorporating the dry ingredients to make a smooth batter. Mix the chocolate and milk in a pan. Heat gently until the chocolate has melted, then beat into the batter until smooth. Stir in the orange rind and juice.

2 Heat a large, heavy-based frying pan or griddle. Grease with a little butter or oil. Drop large spoonfuls of batter on to the hot surface, leaving room for spreading. Cook over a medium heat. When the pancakes are lightly browned underneath and bubbly on top, flip them over to cook the other side. Slide on to a plate and keep hot, then make more in the same way.

3 For the sauce, cut the rind of 1 orange in long shreds and set aside. Peel both oranges, taking care to remove all the pith, then slice the flesh thinly. Heat the butter and sugar in a wide, shallow pan over a low heat, stirring until the sugar dissolves. Stir in the crème fraîche and heat gently.

4 Add the pancakes and orange slices to the sauce, heat gently for 1–2 minutes, then spoon over the liqueur. Sprinkle with the reserved orange rind and the chocolate curls and serve the pancakes immediately.

Nutritional information: Energy 752kcal/3131kJ; Protein 12.1g; Carbohydrate 58.1g, of which sugars 35.5g; Fat 53.2g, of which saturates 27g; Cholesterol 185mg; Calcium 282mg; Fibre 3.9g; Sodium 304mg.

Chocolate chip banana pancakes

These banana-flavoured pancakes are easy to whip up in batches, and are great to serve as a dessert. The flaked almonds on the side add a bit of crunch.

MAKES 16

2 ripe bananas
2 eggs
200ml/7fl oz/scant 1 cup milk
150g/5oz/1¼ cups self-raising (self-rising) flour, sifted
25g/1oz/⅓ cup ground almonds
15ml/1 tbsp caster (superfine) sugar
pinch of salt
15ml/1 tbsp plain (semisweet) chocolate chips
butter, for frying
50g/2oz/½ cup toasted flaked (sliced) almonds

FOR THE TOPPING

150ml/¼ pint/⅔ cup double (heavy) cream
15ml/1 tbsp icing (confectioners') sugar

1 Mash the bananas in a bowl. Beat in the eggs and half the milk. Mix in the flour, ground almonds, sugar and salt. Add the remaining milk and the chocolate chips.

2 Stir the mixture well until it makes a thick batter. Heat a little butter in a non-stick frying pan. Spoon the pancake mixture into heaps, allowing room for them to spread. When the pancakes are lightly browned underneath, flip them over to cook the other side. Slide on to a plate and keep hot, then make more pancakes in the same way.

3 Make the topping. Pour the cream into a bowl. Add the icing sugar and whip to soft peaks. Spoon the cream on to the pancakes and decorate with flaked almonds. Serve.

Nutritional information: Energy 192kcal/798kJ; Protein 3.4g; Carbohydrate 13.7g, of which sugars 6.3g; Fat 14.1g, of which saturates 7.1g; Cholesterol 51mg; Calcium 70mg; Fibre 0.8g; Sodium 89mg.

Prune beignets in chocolate Armagnac sauce

Go on, indulge yourself! Slide your spoon into silky chocolate sauce, scoop up a feather-light prune beignet and get ready for rapture.

SERVES 4

75g/3oz/³/₄ cup plain (all-purpose) flour
45ml/3 tbsp ground almonds
45ml/3 tbsp oil or melted butter
1 egg white
60ml/4 tbsp water
oil, for deep-frying
175g/6oz/³/₄ cup stoned (pitted) prunes
45ml/3 tbsp vanilla sugar
15ml/1 tbsp unsweetened cocoa powder

FOR THE SAUCE
200g/7oz milk chocolate, broken into
    squares
120ml/4fl oz/¹/₂ cup crème fraîche
30ml/2 tbsp Armagnac or brandy

1 Start by making the sauce. Melt the chocolate gently in a heatproof bowl set over a pan of barely simmering water.

2 Remove from the heat, stir in the crème fraîche until smooth, then add the Armagnac or brandy. Replace the bowl over the water (off the heat) to keep warm.

3 Beat the flour, almonds, oil or butter and egg white in a bowl, then beat in enough of the water to make a smooth, thick batter.

4 Heat the oil for deep-frying to 180°C/350°F or until a cube of dried bread browns in 30–45 seconds. Dip the prunes into the batter and fry, a few at a time, until the beignets rise to the surface and are golden brown.

5 Remove each batch with a slotted spoon, drain on kitchen paper and keep hot. Mix the vanilla sugar and cocoa in a bowl, add the beignets and toss well to coat. Serve with the Armagnac sauce.

Nutritional information: Energy 727kcal/3039kJ; Protein 11.3g; Carbohydrate 71.7g, of which sugars 56.5g; Fat 44.1g, of which saturates 24.2g; Cholesterol 69mg; Calcium 209mg; Fibre 4.8g; Sodium 176mg.

Rich chocolate brioche bake

This scrumptious baked dessert may be based on good old bread and butter pudding, but chocolate, brioche and bitter marmalade give it superstar status.

SERVES 4

200g/7oz plain (semisweet) chocolate, broken into squares
60ml/4 tbsp bitter marmalade
45ml/3 tbsp unsalted (sweet) butter
4 individual brioches, or 1 large brioche loaf
3 eggs
300ml/½ pint/1¼ cups milk
300ml/½ pint/1¼ cups single (light) cream
30ml/2 tbsp demerara (raw) sugar

1 Preheat the oven to 180°C/350°F/ Gas 4. Lightly butter a shallow ovenproof dish.

2 Melt the chocolate with the marmalade and butter in a heatproof bowl set over a pan of barely simmering water, stirring the mixture occasionally.

3 Slice the brioche(s), and spread the chocolate mixture over each slice. Arrange so that they overlap in the dish.

4 Beat the eggs, milk and cream in a bowl, then pour over the slices. Sprinkle with the demerara sugar and bake for 40–50 minutes until the custard is lightly set and bubbling. Serve.

Nutritional information: Energy 987kcal/4143kJ; Protein 25.9g; Carbohydrate 127.8g, of which sugars 59.1g; Fat 45g, of which saturates 25.4g; Cholesterol 213mg; Calcium 460mg; Fibre 4.4g; Sodium 1060mg.

Hot mocha rum soufflés

These superb soufflés always rise to the occasion. Serve them as soon as they are cooked, for a fantastic finale to a dinner party. They are delicious served with some fresh berries on the side.

SERVES 6

25g/1oz/2 tbsp unsalted (sweet)
  butter, melted
65g/2¹/₂oz/generous ¹/₂ cup
  unsweetened cocoa powder
75g/3oz/¹/₃ cup caster (superfine) sugar
60ml/4 tbsp strong black coffee
30ml/2 tbsp dark rum
6 egg whites
icing (confectioners') sugar, for dusting

1 Preheat the oven with a baking sheet inside to 190°C/375°F/Gas 5. Grease six 250ml/8fl oz/1-cup soufflé dishes with melted butter.

2 Mix 15ml/1 tbsp of the cocoa with 15ml/1 tbsp of the caster sugar in a bowl. Use the mixture to coat the inside of each greased soufflé dish.

3 Mix the remaining cocoa with the coffee and rum.

4 Whisk the egg whites in a clean, grease-free bowl until they form firm peaks. Whisk in the remaining caster sugar. Stir a generous spoonful of the whites into the cocoa mixture to lighten it, then fold in the remaining whites.

5 Spoon the mixture into the prepared dishes, smoothing the tops. Place on the hot baking sheet, and bake for 12–15 minutes or until well risen. Serve immediately, dusted with icing sugar.

Nutritional information: Energy 148kcal/619kJ; Protein 5g; Carbohydrate 14.3g, of which sugars 13.1g; Fat 5.8g, of which saturates 3.6g; Cholesterol 9mg; Calcium 23mg; Fibre 1.3g; Sodium 190mg..

Easy chocolate and orange soufflé

An inventive twist on a classic recipe. Serve this light and airy soufflé with lashings of cream. Make in smaller, individual dishes to add a touch of class to a dinner party.

SERVES 4

600ml/1 pint/2¹/₂ cups milk
50g/2oz/generous ¹/₄ cup semolina
50g/2oz/¹/₃ cup soft light
  brown sugar
grated rind of 1 orange
90ml/6 tbsp fresh orange juice
3 eggs, separated
65g/2¹/₂oz plain (semisweet)
  chocolate, grated
icing (confectioners') sugar, for sprinkling
single (light) cream, to serve

1 Place a baking sheet in the oven, and preheat it to 200°C/400°F/ Gas 6. Butter a 1.75-litre/3-pint/ 7¹/₂-cup soufflé dish.

2 Pour the milk into a pan, sprinkle over the semolina and brown sugar, then heat, stirring continuously, until boiling and thickened.

3 Remove from the heat. Cool slightly, then beat in the orange rind and juice, egg yolks and all but 15ml/ 1 tbsp of the grated chocolate.

4 In a clean, grease-free bowl, whisk the egg whites until stiff but not dry, then lightly fold into the semolina mixture in three batches. Spoon the mixture into the dish.

5 Place the dish on the baking sheet and bake for about 30 minutes, until just set in the centre and risen.

6 Sprinkle the top with the reserved chocolate and dust with the icing sugar. Serve with cream.

Nutritional information: Energy 308kcal/1300kJ; Protein 12.1g; Carbohydrate 42.1g, of which sugars 32.3g; Fat 11.5g, of which saturates 5.5g; Cholesterol 153mg; Calcium 218mg; Fibre 0.7g; Sodium 123mg.

Hot chocolate cake

This warm, moist cake must surely be the ultimate in comfort food. It looks stunning served with the contrasting creamy white chocolate sauce.

MAKES 10–12 SLICES

200g/7oz/1¾ cups self-raising wholemeal (self-rising whole-wheat) flour
25g/1oz/¼ cup unsweetened cocoa powder
pinch of salt
175g/6oz/¾ cup soft margarine
175g/6oz/1 cup soft light brown sugar
few drops of vanilla extract
4 eggs, beaten
75g/3oz white chocolate, chopped
chocolate leaves and curls, to decorate

FOR THE WHITE CHOCOLATE SAUCE

75g/3oz white chocolate, chopped into small pieces
150ml/¼ pint/⅔ cup single (light) cream
30–45ml/2–3 tbsp milk

1 Preheat the oven to 160°C/325°F/ Gas 3. Sift the flour, cocoa and salt into a bowl, then add the bran remaining in the sieve.

2 In a separate bowl, beat the margarine, sugar and vanilla until fluffy, then beat in the eggs, one at a time, alternately with the flour mixture, to make a smooth mixture.

3 Stir in the chocolate and spoon the mixture into a greased 675–900g/1½–2lb loaf tin (pan).

4 Bake for 30–40 minutes or until just firm to the touch and shrinking away from the sides of the tin.

5 To make the sauce, put the chocolate and cream in a pan and heat very gently until the chocolate is melted. Add the milk and stir until cool.

6 Spoon a little sauce on to each serving plate and add a slice of cake. Decorate with a few chocolate leaves and curls. Serve immediately.

Nutritional information: Energy 343kcal/1432kJ; Protein 5.4g; Carbohydrate 35.7g, of which sugars 23.1g; Fat 20.8g, of which saturates 7.1g; Cholesterol 71mg; Calcium 124mg; Fibre 0.8g; Sodium 221mg.

Steamed chocolate and fruit puddings

Some things always turn out well, including these wonderful puddings. Dark, fluffy chocolate sponge is topped with cranberries and apple, and served with a honeyed chocolate syrup.

SERVES 4

115g/4oz/²/₃ cup dark muscovado
   (molasses) sugar
1 eating apple
75g/3oz/³/₄ cup cranberries
115g/4oz/¹/₂ cup soft margarine
2 eggs
75g/3oz/³/₄ cup plain (all-purpose) flour
2.5ml/¹/₂ tsp baking powder
45ml/3 tbsp unsweetened cocoa powder

FOR THE CHOCOLATE SYRUP

115g/4oz plain (semisweet) chocolate,
   broken into squares
30ml/2 tbsp clear honey
15ml/1 tbsp unsalted (sweet) butter
2.5ml/¹/₂ tsp vanilla extract

1 Prepare a steamer or half-fill a pan with water and bring it to the boil. Grease four individual heatproof bowls and sprinkle each one with a little of the muscovado sugar to coat.

2 Peel and core the apple. Dice it into a bowl, add the cranberries and mix well. Divide among the prepared bowls.

3 Place the remaining muscovado sugar in a large bowl. Add the margarine, eggs, flour, baking powder and cocoa; beat until combined and smooth.

4 Spoon the mixture into the bowls and cover each with a double thickness of foil. Steam for 45 minutes, topping up the steamer or pan with water, until well risen and firm.

5 For the syrup, mix the chocolate, honey, butter and vanilla in a pan. Heat gently, stirring, until melted and smooth. Run a knife around the edge of each pudding to loosen it, then turn out on to plates. Serve with the syrup.

Nutritional information: Energy 672kcal/2811kJ; Protein 8.7g; Carbohydrate 73.1g, of which sugars 57.3g; Fat 40.4g, of which saturates 13.9g; Cholesterol 105mg; Calcium 84mg; Fibre 3.2g; Sodium 366mg.

Rich chocolate and coffee pudding

A delectable blend of coffee and chocolate with a surprising layer of creamy coffee sauce underneath. Add a generous helping of whipped cream for the perfect finish.

SERVES 6

75g/3oz/³/₄ cup plain (all-purpose) flour
10ml/2 tsp baking powder
pinch of salt
50g/2oz/¹/₄ cup butter or margarine
25g/1oz plain (semisweet) chocolate,
   chopped into small pieces
115g/4oz/¹/₂ cup caster (superfine)
   sugar
75ml/3fl oz/5 tbsp milk
1.5ml/¹/₄ tsp vanilla extract
whipped cream, for serving

FOR THE TOPPING

30ml/2 tbsp instant coffee powder
325ml/11fl oz/generous ¹/₂ pint
   hot water
90g/3¹/₂oz/7 tbsp soft dark
   brown sugar
65g/2¹/₂oz/5 tbsp caster
   (superfine) sugar
30ml/2 tbsp unsweetened cocoa
   powder, plus extra for dusting

1 Preheat the oven to 180°C/350°F/Gas 4. Grease a 23cm/9in square non-stick baking tin (pan).

2 Sift the flour, baking powder and salt into a small bowl. Set aside.

3 Melt the butter or margarine, chocolate and caster sugar in a heatproof bowl set over a saucepan of simmering water, or in a double boiler, stirring occasionally. Remove the bowl from the heat.

4 Add the flour mixture and stir well. Stir in the milk and vanilla extract. Mix with a wooden spoon, then pour the mixture into the prepared baking tin.

5 Make the topping. Dissolve the coffee in the water in a bowl. Allow to cool. Mix the brown sugar, caster sugar and cocoa powder in a separate bowl. Sprinkle the mixture over the pudding mixture.

6 Pour the coffee evenly over the surface. Bake for 40 minutes or until the pudding is risen and set on top. The coffee mixture will have formed a delicious creamy sauce underneath. Serve immediately with whipped cream and dust with cocoa powder.

Nutritional information: Energy 325kcal/1371kJ; Protein 3g; Carbohydrate 60.6g, of which sugars 50.5g; Fat 9.5g, of which saturates 5.8g; Cholesterol 19mg; Calcium 66mg; Fibre 1.1g; Sodium 107mg.

Chocolate chip and banana pudding

This comforting dessert is a great choice for an informal dinner party, as it can simply be left to cook while you enjoy the company of your guests.

SERVES 4

200g/7oz/1¾ cups self-raising (self-rising) flour
75g/3oz/6 tbsp unsalted (sweet) butter
2 ripe bananas
75g/3oz/⅓ cup caster (superfine) sugar
60ml/4 tbsp milk
1 egg, beaten
60ml/4 tbsp plain (semisweet) chocolate chips or chopped chocolate
Glossy Chocolate Sauce and whipped cream, to serve

1 Prepare a steamer or half-fill a pan with water and bring it to the boil. Grease a 1-litre/1¾-pint/4-cup heatproof bowl. Sift the flour into another bowl and rub in the butter until the mixture resembles coarse breadcrumbs.

2 Mash the bananas in a bowl. Stir them into the mixture, with the caster sugar. Whisk the milk with the egg in a separate bowl, then beat into the pudding mixture. Stir in the chocolate chips or chopped chocolate.

3 Spoon the mixture into the prepared bowl, cover closely with a double thickness of foil, and steam for 2 hours, topping up the water as required during cooking.

4 Run a knife around the top of the pudding to loosen it, then turn it out on to a serving dish. Serve hot, with the chocolate sauce and whipped cream.

Nutritional information: Energy 528kcal/2220kJ; Protein 8.1g; Carbohydrate 79.3g, of which sugars 40.9g; Fat 22g, of which saturates 13g; Cholesterol 89mg; Calcium 222mg; Fibre 2.5g; Sodium 320mg.

Magic chocolate mud pudding

A popular favourite, which magically separates into a light and luscious sponge and a velvety chocolate sauce. Add a scoop of ice cream for an interesting contrast of hot and cold.

SERVES 4

50g/2oz/4 tbsp butter

200g/7oz/generous 1 cup light
   muscovado (brown) sugar

475ml/16fl oz/2 cups milk

90g/3½oz/scant 1 cup self-raising
   (self-rising) flour

5ml/1 tsp ground cinnamon

75ml/5 tbsp unsweetened cocoa powder

Greek (US strained plain) yogurt or
   vanilla ice cream, to serve

1 Preheat the oven to 180°C/350°F/Gas 4. Lightly grease a 1.5-litre/2½-pint/6-cup ovenproof dish and place on a baking sheet.

2 Place the butter in a pan. Add 115g/4oz/¾ cup of the sugar and 150ml/¼ pint/⅔ cup of the milk. Heat gently, stirring from time to time, until the butter has melted and all the sugar has dissolved. Remove the pan from the heat.

3 Sift the flour, cinnamon and 15ml/1 tbsp of the cocoa into the pan and stir into the mixture, mixing evenly. Pour the mixture into the prepared dish and level the surface.

4 Mix the remaining sugar and cocoa powder in a bowl, then sprinkle over the pudding mixture. Pour the remaining milk over the pudding.

5 Bake for 45–50 minutes or until the sponge has risen to the top and is firm to the touch. Serve hot, with the yogurt or ice cream.

Nutritional information: Energy 480kcal/2025kJ; Protein 10g; Carbohydrate 77.6g, of which sugars 58.3g; Fat 16.7g, of which saturates 10.2g; Cholesterol 34mg; Calcium 227mg; Fibre 3g; Sodium 309mg.

Pears in chocolate fudge blankets

The delicate flavour of warm poached pears swathed in a rich chocolate fudge sauce – who could resist such a sensual pleasure?

SERVES 6

6 ripe eating pears
30ml/2 tbsp lemon juice
75g/3oz/¹⁄₃ cup caster (superfine) sugar
300ml/¹⁄₂ pint/1¹⁄₄ cups water
1 cinnamon stick

FOR THE SAUCE

200ml/7fl oz/scant 1 cup double
    (heavy) cream
150g/5oz/scant 1 cup light muscovado
    (brown) sugar
25g/1oz/2 tbsp unsalted (sweet) butter
60ml/4 tbsp golden (light corn) syrup
120ml/4fl oz/¹⁄₂ cup milk
200g/7oz dark (bittersweet) chocolate,
    broken into squares

1 Peel the pears thinly, leaving the stalks on. Scoop out the cores from the base. Brush the cut surfaces with lemon juice to prevent browning.

2 Place the sugar and water in a large saucepan. Heat gently until the sugar dissolves. Add the pears and cinnamon stick with any remaining lemon juice, and, if necessary, a little more water, so that the pears are almost covered.

3 Bring to the boil, then lower the heat, cover the pan and simmer the pears gently for about 15–20 minutes, or until they are just tender.

4 Meanwhile, make the sauce. Place the cream, sugar, butter, golden syrup and milk in a heavy pan. Heat gently until the sugar has dissolved and the butter and syrup have melted, then bring to the boil. Boil, stirring constantly, for about 5 minutes or until the sauce is thick and smooth. Remove from the heat and stir in the chocolate, a few squares at a time, until melted.

5 Using a slotted spoon, transfer the poached pears to a dish. Keep hot. Boil the cooking liquid rapidly to reduce to about 45–60ml/3–4 tbsp. Remove the cinnamon stick and stir the syrup into the chocolate sauce.

6 Serve the pears on individual plates, with the hot chocolate fudge sauce spooned over.

Nutritional information: Energy 613kcal/2570kJ; Protein 3.6g; Carbohydrate 84.8g, of which sugars 84.5g; Fat 31.2g, of which saturates 19.1g; Cholesterol 58mg; Calcium 90mg; Fibre 4.1g; Sodium 77mg.

Peachy chocolate bake

When summer fruits are in season, you could make this pudding extra special by using fresh, ripe peaches or nectarines, or try it with plums or cherries.

SERVES 6

200g/7oz dark (bittersweet) chocolate, broken into squares
115g/4oz/¹/₂ cup unsalted (sweet) butter
4 eggs, separated
115g/4oz/¹/₂ cup caster (superfine) sugar
425g/15oz can peach slices, drained
whipped cream or natural (plain) yogurt, to serve

1 Preheat the oven to 160°C/325°F/Gas 3. Butter a wide ovenproof dish. Melt the chocolate with the butter in a heatproof bowl set over a pan of barely simmering water. Remove from the heat.

2 In a bowl, whisk the egg yolks with the sugar until thick and pale.

3 In a clean, grease-free bowl, whisk the egg whites until stiff.

4 Beat the chocolate into the egg yolk mixture, then fold in the egg whites lightly and evenly.

5 Fold the peach slices into the mixture, then turn the mixture into the prepared dish.

6 Bake for about 35–40 minutes, or until the pudding is risen and just firm. Serve hot, with whipped cream or natural yogurt.

Nutritional information: Energy 465kcal/1942kJ; Protein 6.5g; Carbohydrate 48.2g, of which sugars 47.9g; Fat 28.8g, of which saturates 16.6g; Cholesterol 170mg; Calcium 47mg; Fibre 1.4g; Sodium 175mg.

Chocolate almond meringue pie

Treat your tastebuds to the contrasting textures and flavours of fluffy meringue on a velvety smooth chocolate filling in a light orange pastry crust.

SERVES 6

175g/6oz/1½ cups plain
   (all-purpose) flour
50g/2oz/⅓ cup ground rice
150g/5oz/⅔ cup unsalted (sweet) butter
finely grated rind of 1 orange
1 egg yolk
flaked (sliced) almonds and melted dark
   (bittersweet) chocolate, to decorate

FOR THE FILLING

150g/5oz dark (bittersweet) chocolate,
   broken into squares
50g/2oz/4 tbsp unsalted (sweet)
   butter, softened
75g/3oz/⅓ cup caster (superfine) sugar
10ml/2 tsp cornflour (cornstarch)
4 egg yolks
75g/3oz/¾ cup ground almonds

FOR THE MERINGUE

3 egg whites
150g/5oz/⅔ cup caster (superfine) sugar

1 Sift the flour and ground rice into a bowl. Rub in the butter, to resemble breadcrumbs. Stir in the orange rind. Add the egg yolk and blend together. Roll out and line a 23cm/9in flan tin (pan). Chill for 30 minutes.

2 Preheat the oven to 190°C/375°F/ Gas 5. Prick the pastry base all over with a fork, cover with baking parchment weighed down with baking beans and bake blind for 10 minutes. Remove from the oven and remove the baking beans and paper.

3 For the filling, melt the chocolate in a heatproof bowl over a pan of simmering water. Cream the butter with the sugar in a bowl, then beat in the cornflour and egg yolks.

4 Fold in the almonds and chocolate. Spread in the pastry case. Bake for 10 minutes.

5 For the meringue, whisk the egg whites until stiff, then gradually whisk in half the caster sugar. Fold in the remaining sugar. Spoon the meringue over the filling, lifting it up with the back of the spoon to form peaks.

6 Reduce the oven temperature to 180°C/350°F/Gas 4 and bake for 15 minutes, until golden. Sprinkle with the almonds, drizzle with melted chocolate and serve immediately.

Nutritional information: Energy 792kcal/3312kJ; Protein 11.4g; Carbohydrate 87g, of which sugars 56g; Fat 46.4g, of which saturates 23.5g; Cholesterol 241mg; Calcium 128mg; Fibre 2.6g; Sodium 248mg.

Chocolate, date and almond filo coil

Experience the allure of the Middle East with this delectable dessert. Crisp filo pastry conceals a chocolate and rosewater filling studded with dates and almonds.

SERVES 6

275g/10oz packet filo pastry, thawed
    if frozen
50g/2oz/4 tbsp unsalted (sweet) butter,
    melted
icing (confectioners') sugar, cocoa powder
    and ground cinnamon, for dusting

FOR THE FILLING

75g/3oz/6 tbsp unsalted (sweet) butter
115g/4oz dark (bittersweet) chocolate,
    broken into squares
115g/4oz/1 cup ground almonds
115g/4oz/²/₃ cup chopped dates
75g/3oz/²/₃ cup icing (confectioners')
    sugar
10ml/2 tsp rosewater
2.5ml/¹/₂ tsp ground cinnamon

1 Preheat the oven to 180°C/350°F/Gas 4. Grease a 22cm/8¹/₂in round cake tin (pan). Make the filling. Melt the butter with the chocolate in a heatproof bowl over barely simmering water, then remove from the heat and stir in the remaining ingredients to make a thick paste. Leave to cool.

2 Lay one sheet of filo on a clean work surface. Brush it with melted butter, then lay a second sheet on top and brush with butter.

3 Roll a handful of the chocolate almond mixture into a long sausage shape and place along one long edge of the layered filo. Roll the pastry tightly around the filling to make a roll.

4 Place the roll around the outside of the tin. Make enough rolls to fill the tin.

5 Brush the coil with the remaining melted butter. Bake for 30–35 minutes until the pastry is golden brown and crisp. Remove the coil from the tin and place it on a plate. Serve warm, dusted with icing sugar, cocoa and cinnamon.

Nutritional information: Energy 543kcal/2267kJ; Protein 8.2g; Carbohydrate 55.4g, of which sugars 32.4g; Fat 33.6g, of which saturates 15g; Cholesterol 46mg; Calcium 108mg; Fibre 3.2g; Sodium 133mg.

Chocolate pecan pie

If you thought pecan pie couldn't be improved upon, just try this gorgeous chocolate one, with its rich orange crust.

SERVES 6

200g/7oz/1¾ cups plain (all-purpose) flour
65g/2½oz/5 tbsp caster (superfine) sugar
90g/3½oz/scant ½ cup unsalted (sweet) butter, softened
1 egg, beaten
finely grated rind of 1 orange

FOR THE FILLING

200g/7oz/¾ cup golden (light corn) syrup
45ml/3 tbsp light muscovado (brown) sugar
150g/5oz plain (semisweet) chocolate, broken into squares
50g/2oz/4 tbsp butter
3 eggs, beaten
5ml/1 tsp vanilla extract
175g/6oz/1½ cups pecan nuts

1 Sift the flour into a bowl and stir in the sugar. Work in the butter evenly with the fingertips until combined.

2 Beat the egg and orange rind in a bowl, then stir into the flour mixture to make a firm dough. Add a little water if the mixture is too dry.

3 Roll out the pastry on a lightly floured surface and use to line a deep, 20cm/8in loose-based flan tin (pan). Chill for 30 minutes.

4 Preheat the oven to 180°C/350°F/Gas 4. Make the filling. Mix the syrup, sugar, chocolate and butter in a small pan. Heat gently until melted.

5 Remove from the heat and beat in the eggs and vanilla extract. Sprinkle the pecan nuts into the pastry case and carefully pour over the chocolate mixture.

6 Place on a baking sheet and bake for 50–60 minutes or until set. Cool in the tin for 10 minutes, then serve.

Nutritional information: Energy 843kcal/3524kJ; Protein 11.6g; Carbohydrate 90.8g, of which sugars 64.8g; Fat 50.8g, of which saturates 19.1g; Cholesterol 178mg; Calcium 112mg; Fibre 3g; Sodium 282mg.

Chocolate amaretti peaches

Guests are bound to be impressed when they are served these soft, sweet peaches filled to the brim with a fragrant mixture of amaretti, chocolate, orange, honey and cinnamon.

SERVES 4

115g/4oz amaretti, crushed
50g/2oz plain (semisweet) chocolate,
    chopped
grated rind of ¹/₂ orange
15ml/1 tbsp clear honey

1.5ml/¹/₄ tsp ground cinnamon
1 egg white, lightly beaten
4 firm ripe peaches
150ml/¹/₄ pint/²/₃ cup white wine
15ml/1 tbsp caster (superfine) sugar
whipped cream, to serve

1 Preheat the oven to 190°C/375°F/Gas 5. Mix together the crushed amaretti, chocolate, orange rind, honey and cinnamon in a large bowl. Add the beaten egg white and mix to bind the mixture.

2 Halve and stone (pit) the peaches and fill the cavities with the chocolate mixture, mounding it up slightly.

3 Arrange the stuffed peaches in a lightly buttered, shallow ovenproof dish, which will just hold the peaches comfortably.

4 Mix the white wine and sugar in a jug (pitcher). Pour the wine mixture around the peaches. Bake for 30–40 minutes until the peaches are tender when tested with a slim metal skewer and the filling is golden.

5 Serve the peaches immediately with a little of the cooking juices spooned over. Offer the whipped cream separately.

Nutritional information: Energy 282kcal/1190kJ; Protein 4.1g; Carbohydrate 47g, of which sugars 34.4g; Fat 7.4g, of which saturates 3.8g; Cholesterol 1mg; Calcium 56mg; Fibre 2.4g; Sodium 117mg.

Chocolate cinnamon cake with banana sauce

This simple-to-bake cake contains the winning combination of chocolate and banana. The addition of ground cinnamon adds extra spice and a wonderful aroma.

SERVES 6

25g/1oz plain (semisweet) chocolate, chopped into small pieces
115g/4oz/1/2 cup unsalted (sweet) butter, at room temperature
15ml/1 tbsp instant coffee powder
5 eggs, separated
225g/8oz/1 cup sugar
115g/4oz/1 cup plain (all-purpose) flour
10ml/2 tsp ground cinnamon

FOR THE SAUCE

4 ripe bananas
45ml/3 tbsp soft light brown sugar
15ml/8oz/1 tbsp fresh lemon juice
175ml/6fl oz/3/4 cup whipping cream
15ml/1 tbsp rum (optional)

1 Preheat the oven to 180°C/350°F/Gas 4. Grease a 20cm/8in round cake tin (pan) lightly with butter. Combine the chocolate and butter in the top of a double boiler or in a heatproof bowl set over a pan of simmering water. Stir until melted. Remove from the heat and stir in the coffee. Set aside.

2 Beat the egg yolks with the sugar until thick and lemon-coloured. Add the chocolate mixture and beat on low speed until just blended.

3 Stir the flour and cinnamon together in a small bowl. In another bowl, beat the egg whites until they hold stiff peaks. Fold a dollop of whites into the chocolate mixture to lighten it. Fold in the remaining whites in three batches, alternating with the sifted flour mixture.

4 Pour the mixture into the prepared tin. Bake for 40–50 minutes or until a skewer inserted in the centre comes out clean. Turn the cake out on to a wire rack. Preheat the grill (broiler).

5 Make the sauce. Slice the bananas into a shallow, flameproof dish. Stir in the brown sugar and lemon juice. Place under the grill for 8 minutes, stirring occasionally, until caramelized.

6 Mash the banana mixture until almost smooth. Turn into a bowl and stir in the cream and rum, if using. Slice the cake and serve with the sauce.

Nutritional information: Energy 642kcal/2691kJ; Protein 8.9g; Carbohydrate 80.9g, of which sugars 64.8g; Fat 33.8g, of which saturates 19.4g; Cholesterol 230mg; Calcium 100mg; Fibre 1.4g; Sodium 186mg

Cold and frozen desserts

Cold desserts mean easy entertaining, as they can mostly be prepared ahead. A rich, dark Chocolate Sorbet with Red Fruits can be made days in advance, ready to scoop and serve with fruit, while Chocolate and Chestnut Pots and Black and White Chocolate Mousse will keep in the refrigerator for the next day.

Raspberry, mascarpone and white chocolate cheesecake

Raspberries and white chocolate are an irresistible combination, especially when teamed with rich mascarpone on a crunchy ginger and pecan nut base.

SERVES 8

50g/2oz/4 tbsp unsalted (sweet) butter
225g/8oz ginger nut biscuits
    (gingersnaps), crushed
50g/2oz/1/2 cup chopped pecan nuts

250g/9oz white chocolate, broken
    into squares
225g/8oz/11/2 cups fresh or
    frozen raspberries

FOR THE FILLING
275g/10oz/11/4 cups mascarpone
175g/6oz/3/4 cup fromage frais or ricotta
2 eggs, beaten
45ml/3 tbsp caster (superfine) sugar

FOR THE TOPPING
115g/4oz/1/2 cup mascarpone
75g/3oz/1/3 cup fromage frais or ricotta
white chocolate curls and raspberries,
    to decorate

1 Preheat the oven to 150°C/300°F/Gas 2. Melt the butter in a pan, then stir in the crushed biscuits and nuts. Press into the base of a 23cm/9in springform cake tin (pan).

2 Make the filling. Beat the mascarpone and fromage frais or ricotta in a bowl, then beat in the eggs and caster sugar until evenly mixed.

3 Melt the white chocolate gently in a heatproof bowl over simmering water, then stir into the cheese mixture with the fresh or frozen raspberries.

4 Turn into the prepared tin and spread evenly, then bake for about 1 hour or until just set. Switch off the oven, but do not remove the cheesecake. Leave it until cold and completely set.

5 Remove the sides of the tin and carefully lift the cheesecake on to a serving plate. Make the topping by mixing the mascarpone and fromage frais or ricotta in a bowl, then spread the mixture over the cheesecake. Decorate with chocolate curls and raspberries.

Nutritional information: Energy 551kcal/2305kJ; Protein 12.8g; Carbohydrate 53.9g, of which sugars 41.4g; Fat 33.1g, of which saturates 17g; Cholesterol 88mg; Calcium 170mg; Fibre 1.4g; Sodium 195mg.

Marbled chocolate cheesecake

A new take on an old favourite, this cheesecake looks and tastes divine. The marbled appearance of the cake is very effective, but incredibly simple to achieve.

SERVES 6

50g/2oz/¹⁄₂ cup unsweetened
  cocoa powder
75ml/5 tbsp hot water
900g/2lb cream cheese, at
  room temperature

200g/7oz/scant 1 cup caster
  (superfine) sugar
4 eggs
5ml/1 tsp vanilla extract
75g/3oz digestive biscuits (graham
  crackers), crushed

1 Preheat oven to 180°C/350°F/Gas 4. Line a 20 x 8cm/8 x 3in cake tin (pan) with baking parchment. Grease the paper.

2 Sift the cocoa powder into a bowl. Pour over the hot water and stir to blend. Beat the cheese until smooth, then beat in the sugar, followed by the eggs, one at a time. Do not overmix.

3 Divide the mixture evenly between two bowls. Stir the chocolate mixture into one bowl, then add the vanilla extract to the remaining mixture.

4 Pour a cup or ladleful of the plain mixture into the centre of the tin; it will spread out into an even layer. Slowly pour over a cupful of chocolate mixture in the centre. Continue to alternate the cake mixtures in this way until both are used up. Draw a thin metal skewer through the cake mixture for a marbled effect.

5 Set the tin in a roasting pan and pour in hot water to come 4cm/1¹⁄₂in up the sides of the cake tin. Bake the cheesecake for about 1¹⁄₂ hours, until the top is golden. (The cake will rise during baking but will sink later.) Cool in the tin on a wire rack.

6 Run a knife around the edge of the cake. Invert a flat plate over the tin and turn out the cake. Sprinkle the crushed biscuits evenly over the cake, gently invert another plate on top, and turn over again. Cover and chill for 3 hours, or preferably overnight.

Nutritional information: Energy 923kcal/3828kJ; Protein 11.3g; Carbohydrate 44.4g, of which sugars 36.5g; Fat 79.3g, of which saturates 47.8g; Cholesterol 274mg; Calcium 206mg; Fibre 1.3g; Sodium 653mg.

Chocolate amaretto marquise

This delightful dessert is bound to turn a few heads. It is infused with delicious amaretto liqueur, and can be made in a round tin if you don't have a heart-shaped one.

SERVES 10–12

15ml/1 tbsp flavourless vegetable oil, such as groundnut (peanut) or sunflower

75g/3oz/7–8 amaretti, finely crushed

25g/1oz/¼ cup unblanched almonds, toasted and finely chopped

450g/1lb dark (bittersweet) or plain (semisweet) chocolate, chopped into small pieces

75ml/5 tbsp amaretto liqueur

75ml/5 tbsp golden (light corn) syrup

475ml/16fl oz/2 cups double (heavy) cream

unsweetened cocoa powder, for dusting

FOR THE AMARETTO CREAM

350ml/12fl oz/1½ cups whipping cream or double (heavy) cream

30–45ml/2–3 tbsp Amaretto di Sarone liqueur

1 Lightly oil a 23cm/9in heart-shaped or springform cake tin (pan). Line the bottom with baking parchment and oil the paper. Combine the crushed amaretti and the chopped almonds. Sprinkle evenly on to the base of the tin.

2 Place the chocolate, amaretto liqueur and golden syrup in a pan over a very low heat. Stir frequently until the chocolate is melted and the mixture is smooth. Remove from the heat and allow to cool for about 6–8 minutes, until the mixture feels just warm to the touch.

3 Pour the cream into a bowl. Whip with a hand-held electric mixer, until it just begins to hold its shape. Stir a large spoonful into the chocolate mixture, to lighten it, then quickly add the remaining cream and gently fold into the chocolate mixture. Pour into the prepared tin, on top of the amaretti and almond mixture. Level the surface. Cover the tin and chill overnight.

4 To unmould, run a thin-bladed sharp knife under hot water and dry carefully. Run the knife around the edge of the tin to loosen the dessert. Place a serving plate over the tin, then invert to unmould. Carefully peel off the paper, replacing any crust that sticks to it, and dust with cocoa powder. In a bowl, whip the cream and amaretto liqueur to soft peaks. Serve separately.

Nutritional information: Energy 589kcal/2444kJ; Protein 3.9g; Carbohydrate 38.2g, of which sugars 35.1g; Fat 46.4g, of which saturates 27.5g; Cholesterol 87mg; Calcium 63mg; Fibre 1.2g; Sodium 57mg.

Chocolate pavlova with passion fruit cream

Passion fruit is aptly named. This superb sweet, made in a smaller size, would be a perfect way to round off a romantic candlelit dinner for two.

SERVES 6

4 egg whites
200g/7oz/scant 1 cup caster (superfine)
    sugar
20ml/4 tsp cornflour (cornstarch)
45ml/3 tbsp unsweetened cocoa powder
5ml/1 tsp vinegar
chocolate leaves, to decorate

FOR THE FILLING

150g/5oz plain (semisweet) chocolate,
    broken into squares
250ml/8fl oz/1 cup double (heavy) cream
150g/5oz/²/₃ cup Greek (US strained
    plain) yogurt
2.5ml/¹/₂ tsp vanilla extract
4 passion fruit

1 Preheat the oven to 140°C/275°F/Gas 1. Cut a piece of baking parchment to fit a baking sheet. Draw a 23cm/9in circle on the paper and place it upside down on the baking sheet.

2 Whisk the egg whites in a clean, grease-free bowl until stiff. Gradually whisk in the sugar and continue to whisk until the mixture is stiff again. Whisk in the cornflour, cocoa and vinegar. Spread the mixture over the marked circle, making a slight dip in the centre. Bake for 1¹/₂–2 hours, until golden. Cool on the baking sheet, then remove the paper.

3 For the filling, melt the chocolate in a heatproof bowl set over a pan of simmering water, then remove from the heat and cool slightly. In a separate bowl, whip the cream with the yogurt and vanilla extract until thick. Fold 60ml/4 tbsp into the chocolate, then set both mixtures aside.

4 Halve all the passion fruit and scoop out the pulp. Stir half into the plain cream mixture. Place the meringue on a large serving plate.

5 Fill with the passion fruit cream, then spoon over the chocolate mixture and the remaining passion fruit. Decorate with chocolate leaves and serve.

Nutritional information: Energy 541kcal/2260kJ; Protein 7.3g; Carbohydrate 56.4g, of which sugars 52.3g; Fat 33.6g, of which saturates 20.4g; Cholesterol 59mg; Calcium 96mg; Fibre 1.9g; Sodium 146mg.

Double chocolate snowball

A wonderful treat for the festive season, this unusual cake is infused with liqueur for that subtle orange aroma – definitely one to be kept out of reach of children!

SERVES 12–14

350g/12oz plain (semisweet)
   chocolate, chopped
350g/12oz/1¾ cups caster
   (superfine) sugar
275g/10oz/1¼ cups unsalted (sweet)
   butter, cut into small pieces
8 eggs
60ml/4 tbsp orange-flavoured liqueur
   or brandy
unsweetened cocoa powder, for dusting

FOR THE WHITE CHOCOLATE CREAM

200g/7oz white chocolate, chopped into
   small pieces
475ml/16fl oz/2 cups double (heavy) or
   whipping cream
15ml/1 tbsp orange-flavoured
   liqueur (optional)

1 Preheat the oven to 180°C/350°F/Gas 4. Carefully line a 1.75-litre/3-pint/7½-cup round ovenproof bowl with foil, smoothing the sides. Place the plain chocolate in a heatproof bowl set over a pan of simmering water. Add the caster sugar and stir until the chocolate has melted and the sugar has dissolved. Strain the mixture into a medium bowl.

2 With a hand-held electric mixer at low speed, beat in the butter, then the eggs, one at a time, beating well after each addition. Stir in the liqueur or brandy and pour into the prepared bowl. Tap the sides of the bowl gently to release any large air bubbles.

3 Bake for 1¼–1½ hours until the surface is firm and slightly risen, but cracked. The centre will still be wobbly, but will set on cooling. Remove the bowl to a rack to cool to room temperature; the top will sink. Cover the surface of the bowl with a dinner plate, then cover with foil and chill overnight.

4 To unmould, remove the foil, lift off the plate, and place an upturned serving plate over the top of the bowl. Invert the bowl on to the plate and shake firmly to release the cake. Carefully peel off the foil used for lining the bowl. Cover until ready to decorate.

5 In a food processor fitted with a metal blade, process the white chocolate until fine. Heat 120ml/4fl oz/½ cup of the cream in a small pan until just beginning to simmer. With the food processor running, pour the hot cream through the feeder tube and process until the chocolate has melted completely. Strain into a medium bowl and cool to room temperature, stirring occasionally.

6 In another bowl, beat the remaining cream with the electric mixer until soft peaks form. Add the liqueur, if using, and beat for 30 seconds or until the cream holds its shape, but is not yet stiff. Fold a spoonful of cream into the chocolate mixture to lighten it, then fold in the rest. Spoon into a piping bag fitted with a star tip and pipe rosettes over the surface of the cake. Dust lightly with cocoa powder to finish the decoration.

Nutritional information: Energy 640kcal/2661kJ; Protein 6.7g; Carbohydrate 46.2g, of which sugars 46g; Fat 49g, of which saturates 29.3g; Cholesterol 199mg; Calcium 94mg; Fibre 0.6g; Sodium 185mg.

Devilish chocolate roulade

A decadent dessert for a party or a dinner à deux: the roulade can be made a day or two ahead, then filled and rolled on the day of serving.

SERVES 6–8

175g/6oz dark (bittersweet) chocolate,
   broken into squares
4 eggs, separated
115g/4oz/½ cup caster (superfine) sugar
chocolate-dipped strawberries,
   to decorate
unsweetened cocoa powder, for dusting

FOR THE FILLING

225g/8oz plain (semisweet) chocolate,
   broken into squares
45ml/3 tbsp brandy
2 eggs, separated
250g/9oz/generous 1 cup mascarpone

1 Preheat the oven to 180°C/350°F/Gas 4. Grease a 33 x 23cm/13 x 9in Swiss roll tin (jelly roll pan) and line with baking parchment. Melt the chocolate in a heatproof bowl set over a pan of simmering water. Whisk the egg yolks and sugar in a bowl until pale and thick, then stir in the melted chocolate evenly.

2 In a clean bowl, whisk the egg whites until they form soft peaks, then fold into the chocolate mixture. Spoon into the tin. Bake for 15 minutes until risen and firm to the touch. Dust a sheet of baking parchment with cocoa. Turn the sponge out on the parchment, cover with a dish towel and cool.

3 For the filling, melt the chocolate and brandy in a heatproof bowl set over a pan of hot water. Remove from the heat. Beat the egg yolks, then beat into the chocolate. Whisk the whites to soft peaks, then fold into the filling.

4 Uncover the roulade, remove the paper and spread with half the mascarpone. Spread the chocolate mixture on top. Roll up from a long side to enclose the filling. Transfer to a plate, top with the remaining mascarpone and the chocolate-dipped strawberries and dust with cocoa powder. Chill before serving.

Nutritional information: Energy 486kcal/2022kJ; Protein 10.2g; Carbohydrate 32.8g, of which sugars 32.4g; Fat 34.5g, of which saturates 19.9g; Cholesterol 189mg; Calcium 41mg; Fibre 1.3g; Sodium 143mg.

Tiramisù in chocolate cups

Give in to the temptation of tiramisù, with its magical mocha flavour. Served in irresistible individual chocolate cups, it is bound to be a talking point at any dinner party.

SERVES 6

1 egg yolk
30ml/2 tbsp caster (superfine) sugar
2.5ml/¹/₂ tsp vanilla extract
250g/9oz/generous 1 cup mascarpone
15ml/1 tbsp unsweetened cocoa powder
120ml/4fl oz/¹/₂ cup strong black coffee
30ml/2 tbsp coffee liqueur
16 amaretti, roughly broken
unsweetened cocoa powder, for dusting

FOR THE CHOCOLATE CUPS

175g/6oz plain (semisweet) chocolate,
 broken into squares
25g/1oz/2 tbsp unsalted (sweet) butter

1 Make the chocolate cups. Cut out six 15cm/6in rounds of baking parchment. Melt the chocolate with the butter in a heatproof bowl over barely simmering water. Stir until smooth, then spread a spoonful of the chocolate mixture over each circle, to within 2cm/³/₄in of the edge.

2 Carefully lift each paper round and drape it over an upturned teacup or ramekin so that the edges curve into frills. Leave until completely set, then carefully lift off and peel away the paper to reveal the chocolate cups.

3 Make the filling. Beat the egg yolk and sugar in a bowl until smooth, then stir in the vanilla and mascarpone. Mix to a smooth creamy consistency.

4 In a separate bowl, blend the cocoa to a paste with a little coffee, then mix with the remaining coffee and liqueur. Stir in the broken amaretti. Place the chocolate cups on individual plates. Divide half the biscuit mixture among them, then spoon over half the mascarpone mixture.

5 Spoon over the remaining biscuit mixture, top with the rest of the mascarpone mixture and dust with cocoa. Chill for 30 minutes before serving.

Nutritional information: Energy 351kcal/1469kJ; Protein 6.9g; Carbohydrate 34.5g, of which sugars 29.6g; Fat 20.4g, of which saturates 12.1g; Cholesterol 62mg; Calcium 33mg; Fibre 1.2g; Sodium 86mg.

Chocolate orange marquise

There are people who quite like chocolate, others who enjoy it now and again, and some who are passionate about the stuff. If you fall into the final category, you'll adore this delectable dessert.

SERVES 6–8

200g/7oz/scant 1 cup caster (superfine) sugar

60ml/4 tbsp freshly squeezed orange juice

350g/12oz dark (bittersweet) chocolate, broken into squares

225g/8oz/1 cup unsalted (sweet) butter, cubed

5 eggs

finely grated rind of 1 orange

45ml/3 tbsp plain (all-purpose) flour

icing (confectioners') sugar and finely pared strips of orange rind, to decorate

1 Preheat the oven to 180°C/350°F/Gas 4. Grease a 23cm/9in round cake tin (pan) with a depth of 6cm/2¹/₂in. Line the base with baking parchment.

2 Place 115g/4oz/¹/₂ cup of the sugar in a pan. Add the orange juice and stir over a gentle heat until the sugar has dissolved completely.

3 Remove from the heat and stir in the chocolate until melted, then add the butter, cube by cube, until melted.

4 Whisk the eggs with the remaining sugar in a large bowl until pale and very thick. Add the orange rind. Then, using a metal spoon, fold the chocolate mixture lightly and evenly into the egg mixture. Sift the flour over the top and fold in evenly.

5 Scrape the mixture into the prepared tin. Place in a roasting pan, transfer to the oven, then pour hot water into the roasting pan to reach about halfway up the sides of the cake tin.

6 Bake for 1 hour or until the cake is firm to the touch. Remove the tin from the roasting pan and cool for 15–20 minutes. Turn the cake out on to a serving plate and leave to cool completely, then chill. Dust with icing sugar and decorate with strips of pared orange rind before serving.

Nutritional information: Energy 553kcal/2309kJ; Protein 3.1g; Carbohydrate 59.1g, of which sugars 54.4g; Fat 35.5g, of which saturates 22g; Cholesterol 63mg; Calcium 41mg; Fibre 1.3g; Sodium 176mg.

Chocolate, banana and toffee pie

Chocoholics love finding new ways of using their favourite ingredient. Here's how it can help to make the famous Banoffee Pie even more delicious.

SERVES 6

65g/2½oz/5 tbsp unsalted (sweet)
   butter
250g/9oz milk chocolate digestive
   biscuits (graham crackers)
chocolate curls, to decorate

FOR THE FILLING

397g/13oz can sweetened condensed
   milk
150g/5oz plain (semisweet) chocolate,
   broken into squares
120ml/4fl oz/½ cup crème fraîche or
   single (light) cream
15ml/1 tbsp golden (light corn) syrup

FOR THE TOPPING

2 bananas
250ml/8fl oz/1 cup crème fraîche
10ml/2 tbsp strong black coffee

1 Melt the butter in a pan. Crush the biscuits quite finely in a food processor or with a rolling pin. Place them in a bowl and stir in the melted butter. Press on to the base and sides of a 23cm/9in loose-based flan tin (pan). Leave to set.

2 For the filling, place the unopened can of condensed milk in a pan of boiling water and cover with a lid. Lower the heat and simmer for 2 hours, topping up the water as necessary. Do not allow to boil dry. Remove from the heat and set aside, covered, until the can has cooled down completely in the water. Do not open the can until it is completely cold.

3 Melt the chocolate with the crème fraîche and golden syrup in a heatproof bowl set over a pan of simmering water. Stir in the caramelized condensed milk and beat until mixed, then spread the filling over the biscuit crust. Slice the bananas and arrange them over the filling.

4 Stir together the crème fraîche and coffee, then spoon over the bananas. Decorate liberally with the chocolate curls and chill before serving.

Nutritional information: Energy 900kcal/3758kJ; Protein 11.5g; Carbohydrate 90g, of which sugars 73.2g; Fat 57.4g, of which saturates 35.8g; Cholesterol 139mg; Calcium 275mg; Fibre 1.8g; Sodium 368mg.

Chocolate pecan torte

Nuts and chocolate always go well together. The chocolate honey glaze and the tempting toasted pecans on top of this torte make it simply irresistible.

SERVES 16

200g/7oz dark (bittersweet) chocolate, chopped into small pieces

150g/5oz/10 tbsp unsalted (sweet) butter, cut into pieces

4 eggs

90g/3½oz/scant ½ cup caster (superfine) sugar

10ml/2 tsp vanilla extract

115g/4oz/1 cup ground pecan nuts

10ml/2 tsp ground cinnamon

24 toasted pecan halves, to decorate

FOR THE CHOCOLATE HONEY GLAZE

115g/4oz dark (bittersweet) chocolate, chopped into small pieces

50g/2oz/¼ cup unsalted (sweet) butter, cut into pieces

30ml/2 tbsp clear honey

pinch of ground cinnamon

1 Preheat the oven to 180°C/350°F/Gas 4. Grease a 20 x 5cm/8 x 2in springform tin (pan) and line with baking parchment. Wrap the tin in foil to prevent water from seeping in. Melt the chocolate and butter, stirring until smooth. Beat the eggs, sugar and vanilla in a bowl until the mixture is frothy. Stir in the melted chocolate, ground nuts and cinnamon. Pour into the tin.

2 Place the tin in a roasting pan. Pour in boiling water to come 2cm/¾in up the side of the springform tin. Bake for 25–30 minutes until the edge of the cake is set but the centre is still soft. Remove from the water bath and lift off the foil. Cool in the tin on a wire rack.

3 Heat all the glaze ingredients in a small pan until melted, stirring until smooth. Off the heat, half-dip the toasted pecan halves in the glaze and place on a baking sheet lined with baking parchment until set.

4 Remove the cake from the tin, place on the rack and pour the remaining glaze over. Decorate the torte with chocolate-dipped pecans and leave to set. Transfer to a plate when ready to serve, and slice into wedges.

Nutritional information: Energy 308kcal/1282kJ; Protein 3.6g; Carbohydrate 20.5g, of which sugars 20.1g; Fat 24.2g, of which saturates 10.8g; Cholesterol 75mg; Calcium 25mg; Fibre 1g; Sodium 95mg.

Rich chocolate berry tart
with blackberry sauce

This is a berry tart with a difference. Make it filled with creamy chocolate ganache and served with a tangy blackberry sauce in the summer or autumn, when berries are readily available.

SERVES 10

115g/4oz/¹/₂ cup unsalted (sweet) butter, softened

115g/4oz/¹/₂ cup caster (superfine) sugar

2.5ml/¹/₂ tsp salt

15ml/1 tbsp vanilla extract

50g/2oz/¹/₂ cup unsweetened cocoa powder

175g/6oz/1¹/₂ cups plain (all-purpose) flour

450g/1lb fresh berries, for topping

FOR THE CHOCOLATE GANACHE FILLING

475ml/16fl oz/2 cups double (heavy) cream

150g/5oz/¹/₂ cup blackberry or raspberry jelly

225g/8oz dark (bittersweet) chocolate, chopped into small pieces

25g/1oz/2 tbsp unsalted (sweet) butter, cut into small pieces

FOR THE BLACKBERRY SAUCE

225g/8oz blackberries or raspberries

15ml/1 tbsp lemon juice

30ml/2 tbsp caster (superfine) sugar

30ml/2 tbsp blackberry- or raspberry-flavoured liqueur

1 In a food processor fitted with a metal blade, process the butter, sugar, salt and vanilla until creamy. Add the cocoa and process for 1 minute. Add the flour all at once, then pulse for 10–15 seconds.

2 Place a piece of clear film (plastic wrap) on the work surface. Turn the dough out on to this, shape into a flat disc and wrap tightly. Chill for 1 hour.

3 Lightly grease a 23-cm/9-in flan tin (pan) with a removable base. Let the dough soften for 5–10 minutes, then roll out between two sheets of clear film to a 28cm/11in round, about 5mm/¹/₄in thick.

4 Carefully peel off the top sheet of clear film and invert the dough into the prepared tin. Ease the dough into the tin, and when in position lift off the clear film. With floured fingers, press the dough on to the base and sides of the tin, then roll the rolling pin over the edge to cut off any excess dough. Prick the base of the dough with a fork. Chill for 1 hour.

5 Preheat the oven to 180°C/350°F/Gas 4. Line the pastry case with baking parchment and fill with baking beans. Bake blind for 10 minutes. Remove the paper and beans and bake for 5 minutes more, until the pastry is just set. Cool in the tin on a wire rack.

6 For the ganache filling, bring the cream and berry jelly to the boil in a pan, stirring. Remove from the heat and add the chocolate all at once, stirring until melted and smooth. Stir in the butter until melted, then strain into the cooled tart shell, smoothing the top. Cool the tart completely.

7 Prepare the sauce. Process the berries, lemon juice and sugar in a food processor until smooth. Strain into a small bowl and add the liqueur.

8 To serve, remove the tart from the tin. Place on a serving plate and arrange the berries on top of the tart. With a pastry brush, brush the berries with a little of the blackberry sauce to glaze lightly. Chill for 30 minutes. Serve the remaining sauce separately.

Nutritional information: Energy 653kcal/2722kJ; Protein 6g; Carbohydrate 58.9g, of which sugars 41.8g; Fat 44.9g, of which saturates 27.7g; Cholesterol 96mg; Calcium 95mg; Fibre 3.5g; Sodium 152mg.

Mississippi mud pie

Mud, mud, glorious mud – isn't that what the song says? Well, you can't get much more glorious than this – its status as a popular classic is definitely well earned.

SERVES 6–8

250g/9oz/2¼ cups plain
  (all-purpose) flour
150g/5oz/²⁄₃ cup unsalted (sweet) butter
2 egg yolks
15–30ml/1–2 tbsp iced water

FOR THE FILLING
3 eggs, separated
20ml/4 tsp cornflour (cornstarch)
75g/3oz/¹⁄₃ cup caster (superfine) sugar
400ml/14fl oz/1¾ cups milk

150g/5oz plain (semisweet) chocolate,
  broken into squares
5ml/1 tsp vanilla extract
1 sachet powdered gelatine
45ml/3 tbsp water
30ml/2 tsp dark rum

FOR THE TOPPING
175g/6fl oz/¾ cup double (heavy)
  cream, whipped
chocolate curls, to decorate

1 Sift the flour into a bowl and rub in the butter until the mixture resembles coarse breadcrumbs. Stir in the egg yolks with just enough iced water to bind the mixture to a soft dough. Roll out on a lightly floured surface and line a deep 23cm/9in flan tin (pan). Chill for about 30 minutes.

2 Preheat the oven to 190°C/375°F/Gas 5. Prick the pastry with a fork, cover with baking parchment weighed down with baking beans and bake blind for 10 minutes. Remove the baking beans and paper, return to the oven and bake for a further 10 minutes, until the pastry is crisp and golden. Cool in the tin.

3 For the filling, mix the egg yolks, cornflour and 30ml/2 tbsp of the sugar in a bowl. Heat the milk in a pan until almost boiling, then beat into the egg mixture. Return to a clean pan and stir over a low heat until the custard is smooth and thick. Pour half the custard into a bowl. Melt the chocolate in a heatproof bowl over simmering water, then stir into the custard in the bowl, with the vanilla extract. Spread in the pastry case, cover closely to prevent the formation of a skin, cool, then chill until set.

4 Sprinkle the gelatine over the water in a heatproof bowl, leave until spongy, then place over simmering water until all the gelatine has dissolved. Stir into the remaining custard, with the rum. Whisk the egg whites until stiff peaks form, whisk in the remaining sugar, then fold quickly into the custard before it sets. Spoon over the chocolate custard. Chill until set, then remove the pie from the tin and place on a serving plate. Spread whipped cream over the top and sprinkle with chocolate curls.

Nutritional information: Energy 571kcal/2385kJ; Protein 9.4g; Carbohydrate 53.5g, of which sugars 22.7g; Fat 36.2g, of which saturates 21.2g; Cholesterol 196mg; Calcium 160mg; Fibre 1.3g; Sodium 180mg.

Greek chocolate mousse tartlets

Don't be fooled by the filling – it may be based on yogurt, but it's just as sinful as all the other sweet sensations in this collection!

SERVES 6

1 quantity Chocolate Shortcrust Pastry
melted dark (bittersweet) chocolate, to
   decorate

FOR THE FILLING
200g/7oz white chocolate, broken
   into squares
120ml/4fl oz/¹/₂ cup milk
10ml/2 tsp powdered gelatine
30ml/2 tbsp caster (superfine) sugar
5ml/1 tsp vanilla extract
2 eggs, separated
250g/9oz/generous 1 cup
   Greek (US strained plain) yogurt

1 Preheat the oven to 190°C/375°F/Gas 5. Roll out the pastry and line six deep 10cm/4in loose-based flan tins (pans). Prick the base of each pastry case all over with a fork, cover with baking parchment weighed down with baking beans and bake blind for 10 minutes. Remove the baking beans and paper, return to the oven and bake for a further 15 minutes, or until the pastry is firm. Cool completely in the tins.

2 For the filling, melt the chocolate in a heatproof bowl over simmering water. Pour the milk into a pan, sprinkle over the powdered gelatine and heat gently, stirring, until the gelatine has dissolved completely. Remove from the heat and stir in the chocolate.

3 Whisk the sugar, vanilla extract and egg yolks in a large bowl, then beat in the chocolate mixture. Beat in the yogurt until evenly mixed. Chill until beginning to set. Whisk the egg whites in a clean, grease-free bowl until stiff, then fold into the mixture. Divide among the pastry cases and leave to set. Drizzle the melted chocolate over the tartlets to decorate.

Nutritional information: Energy 555kcal/2320kJ; Protein 11.9g; Carbohydrate 55g, of which sugars 32.2g; Fat 34g, of which saturates 19.7g; Cholesterol 105mg; Calcium 242mg; Fibre 1.5g; Sodium 263mg.

Chocolate lemon tart

If you're looking for something light but with a tangy kick, you'll love this sweet and creamy lemon tart. Perfect for a warm summer's afternoon.

SERVES 8–10

175g/6oz/1½ cups plain
   (all-purpose) flour
10ml/2 tsp unsweetened cocoa powder
25g/1oz/²⁄₄ cup icing
   (confectioners') sugar
2.5ml/½ tsp salt
115g/4oz/½ cup unsalted (sweet)
   butter or margarine
15ml/1 tbsp water
chocolate curls, to decorate

FOR THE FILLING

225g/8oz/1 cup caster (superfine) sugar
6 eggs
grated rind of 2 lemons
175ml/6fl oz/¾ cup fresh lemon juice
175ml/6fl oz/¾ cup double (heavy) or
   whipping cream

1 Grease a 25cm/10in flan tin (pan). Sift the flour, cocoa, icing sugar and salt into a bowl. Set aside. Melt the butter or margarine and water in a pan over a low heat. Pour over the flour mixture and stir until the flour has absorbed all the liquid and the dough is smooth.

2 Press the dough evenly over the base and sides of the prepared tin. Chill the pastry case.

3 Preheat the oven to 190°C/375°F/Gas 5, and place a baking sheet inside to heat up. Prepare the filling. Whisk the sugar and eggs in a bowl until the sugar has dissolved. Add the lemon rind and juice and mix well. Stir in the cream. Taste and add more lemon juice or sugar, if needed, for a sweet taste with a touch of tartness.

4 Pour the filling into the tart shell and place the tin on the hot baking sheet. Bake for 20–25 minutes or until the filling is set. Cool in the tin on a wire rack, then chill. Remove from the tin and decorate with the chocolate curls.

Nutritional information: Energy 379kcal/1585kJ; Protein 6.1g; Carbohydrate 40.5g, of which sugars 27g; Fat 22.6g, of which saturates 12.9g; Cholesterol 163mg; Calcium 68mg; Fibre 0.7g; Sodium 127mg.

Chocolate tiramisù tart

Coffee fans will love this decadent, creamy tart. The filling makes it very rich, so it is best served in small wedges with cups of espresso.

SERVES 12–16

115g/4oz/1/2 cup unsalted
   (sweet) butter
15ml/1 tbsp coffee liqueur
175g/6oz/11/2 cups plain
   (all-purpose) flour
25g/1oz/1/4 cup unsweetened
   cocoa powder
25g/1oz/1/4 cup icing
   (confectioners') sugar
pinch of salt
2.5ml/1/2 tsp vanilla extract
cocoa powder, for dusting
chocolate-coated coffee beans,
   to decorate

FOR THE CHOCOLATE LAYER

350ml/12fl oz/11/2 cups double
   (heavy) cream
15ml/1 tbsp golden (light corn) syrup
115g/4oz dark (bittersweet) chocolate,
   chopped into small pieces
25g/1oz/2 tbsp unsalted (sweet) butter,
   cut into small pieces
30ml/2 tbsp coffee liqueur

FOR THE FILLING

250ml/8fl oz/1 cup whipping cream
350g/12oz/11/2 cups mascarpone, at
   room temperature
45ml/3 tbsp icing (confectioners') sugar
45ml/3 tbsp cold espresso
45ml/3 tbsp coffee liqueur
90g/31/2oz plain (semisweet)
   chocolate, grated

1 Lightly grease a 23cm/9in springform tin (pan). In a pan, heat the butter and liqueur until the butter has melted. Sift the flour, cocoa, icing sugar and salt into a bowl. Remove the butter mixture from the heat, stir in the vanilla extract and gradually stir into the flour mixture until a soft dough forms.

2 Knead lightly until smooth. Press on to the base and up the sides of the tin to within 2cm/3/4in of the top. Prick the dough. Chill for 40 minutes. Preheat the oven to 190°C/375°F/Gas 5. Bake the pastry case for 10 minutes. If the pastry puffs up, prick it with a fork and bake for 3 minutes more until set. Cool in the tin on a rack.

3 For the chocolate layer, bring the cream and syrup to the boil in a pan over a medium heat. Off the heat, add the chocolate, stirring until melted. Beat in the butter and liqueur and pour into the pastry case. Cool completely, then chill.

4 For the filling, using a hand-held electric mixer, whip the cream in a bowl until soft peaks form. In another bowl, beat the cheese until soft, then beat in the icing sugar until smooth and creamy. Gradually beat in the coffee and liqueur; gently fold in the whipped cream and chocolate.

5 Spoon the filling into the pastry case, on top of the chocolate layer. Level the surface. Chill until ready to serve.

6 To serve, run a sharp knife around the side of the tin to loosen the tart shell. Remove the side of the tin and slide the tart on to a plate. Sift a layer of cocoa powder over the tart to decorate, or pipe rosettes of whipped cream around the rim and top each with a chocolate-coated coffee bean.

Nutritional information: Energy 399kcal/1657kJ; Protein 4.8g; Carbohydrate 24.4g, of which sugars 15.8g; Fat 30.9g, of which saturates 20.4g; Cholesterol 60mg; Calcium 49mg; Fibre 0.9g; Sodium 86mg.

Black bottom pie

A devilish chocolate filling topped with smooth rum-flavoured custard gives this totally wicked creation – an American favourite – its unusual name.

SERVES 6–8

250g/9oz/2¼ cups plain
   (all-purpose) flour
150g/5oz/²/₃ cup unsalted
   (sweet) butter
2 egg yolks
15–30ml/1–2 tbsp iced water

FOR THE FILLING
3 eggs, separated
20ml/4 tsp cornflour (cornstarch)
75g/3oz/6 tbsp golden caster
   (superfine) sugar

400ml/14fl oz/1²/₃ cups milk
150g/5oz plain (semisweet) chocolate,
   chopped into small pieces
5ml/1 tsp vanilla extract
1 sachet powdered gelatine
45ml/3 tbsp water
30ml/2 tbsp dark rum

FOR THE TOPPING
175ml/6 fl oz/³/₄ cup double
   (heavy) cream
chocolate curls, to decorate

1 Sift the flour into a bowl and rub in the butter until the mixture resembles coarse breadcrumbs. Stir in the egg yolks with just enough iced water to bind the mixture to a soft dough. Roll out on a lightly floured surface and line a deep 23cm/9in flan tin (pan). Chill the pastry case for 30 minutes.

2 Preheat the oven to 190°C/375°F/Gas 5. Prick the pastry case all over with a fork, cover with baking parchment weighed down with baking beans and bake blind for 10 minutes. Remove the baking beans and paper, return the pastry case to the oven and bake for a further 10 minutes, until the pastry is crisp and golden. Cool in the tin.

3 Make the filling. Mix the egg yolks, cornflour and 30ml/2 tbsp of the sugar in a bowl. Heat the milk in a pan until almost boiling, then beat into the egg mixture. Return to the clean pan and stir over a low heat until the custard has thickened and is smooth. Pour half the custard into a bowl.

4 Put the chocolate in a heatproof bowl. Place over a saucepan of barely simmering water until the chocolate has melted, stirring occasionally until smooth. Stir the melted chocolate into the custard in the bowl, with the vanilla extract. Spread the filling in the pastry case and cover closely with dampened baking parchment or clear film (plastic wrap) to prevent the formation of a skin. Allow to cool, then chill until set.

5 Sprinkle the gelatine over the water in a heatproof bowl, leave until spongy, then place the bowl over a pan of simmering water until all the gelatine has dissolved. Stir into the remaining custard, then add the rum. Whisk the egg whites in a clean, grease-free bowl until peaks form. Whisk in the remaining sugar, a little at a time, until stiff, then fold the egg whites into the rum-flavoured custard.

6 Spoon the rum-flavoured custard over the chocolate layer in the pastry case. Using a spatula, level the mixture, making sure that none of the chocolate custard is visible. Return the pie to the refrigerator until the top layer has set, then remove the pie from the tin and place it on a serving plate. Whip the cream, spread it over the pie and sprinkle with chocolate curls.

Nutritional information: Energy 545kcal/2276kJ; Protein 9.3g; Carbohydrate 51.3g, of which sugars 25.1g; Fat 34.2g, of which saturates 20g; Cholesterol 189mg; Calcium 148mg; Fibre 1.4g; Sodium 173mg.

Black and white chocolate mousse

Dark and dreamy or white and creamy – if you can't decide which mousse you prefer, here is the perfect solution. Why not have both together!

SERVES 8

200g/7oz white chocolate, broken
    into squares
60ml/4 tbsp white rum
30ml/2 tbsp coconut cream
1 egg yolk
60ml/4 tbsp caster (superfine) sugar
250ml/8fl oz/1 cup double (heavy) cream
2 egg whites

FOR THE BLACK MOUSSE

200g/7oz plain (semisweet) chocolate,
    broken into squares
30ml/2 tbsp unsalted (sweet) butter
60ml/4 tbsp dark rum
3 eggs, separated
chocolate curls, to decorate

1 Melt the white chocolate with the rum and coconut cream in a heatproof bowl over barely simmering water. Remove from the heat.

2 Beat the egg yolk and sugar in a separate bowl, then whisk into the chocolate mixture. Whip the cream until it begins to hold its shape, then carefully fold it into the chocolate mixture.

3 Whisk the egg whites in a bowl until they form soft peaks, then fold quickly and evenly into the chocolate mixture. Chill until cold and set.

4 For the dark chocolate mousse, melt the chocolate with the butter and rum in a heatproof bowl over barely simmering water. Remove from the heat and beat in the egg yolks.

5 Whisk the egg whites to soft peaks, then fold them quickly and evenly into the chocolate mixture. Chill until cold and set.

6 Spoon the white and dark chocolate mixtures alternately into tall glasses or into one large glass serving bowl. Decorate with chocolate curls and serve.

Nutritional information: Energy 569kcal/2366kJ; Protein 7.5g; Carbohydrate 39.1g, of which sugars 38.9g; Fat 39.9g, of which saturates 24.2g; Cholesterol 149mg; Calcium 111mg; Fibre 0.6g; Sodium 103mg.

Chocolate truffle tart

A silky chocolate truffle filling gives this tart a truly luxurious feeling. Serve with a large dollop of cream on the side for extra indulgence.

SERVES 12

115g/4oz/1 cup plain (all-purpose) flour
30g/1¼oz/⅓ cup unsweetened
    cocoa powder
50g/2oz/¼ cup caster (superfine) sugar
2.5ml/½ tsp salt
115g/4oz/½ cup unsalted (sweet)
    butter, cut into pieces
1 egg yolk
15–30ml/1–2 tbsp iced water
25g/1oz white or milk chocolate, melted
whipped cream, for serving (optional)

FOR THE TRUFFLE FILLING

350ml/12fl oz/1½ cups double
    (heavy) cream
350g/12oz couverture or dark
    (bittersweet) chocolate, chopped
50g/2oz/4 tbsp unsalted (sweet) butter,
    cut into small pieces
30ml/2 tbsp brandy or liqueur

1 Sift the flour and cocoa into a bowl. In a food processor, process the flour mixture with the sugar and salt. Add the butter and process for 20 seconds, until the mixture resembles coarse breadcrumbs. Beat the egg yolk with the iced water. Add to the flour and pulse until the dough sticks together. Turn out on to clear film (plastic wrap) and shape into a disc. Wrap and chill for 2 hours, until firm. Grease a 23cm/9in tart tin (pan) with a removable base.

2 Let the dough soften briefly, then roll out between sheets of clear film to a 28cm/11in round, 5mm/¼in thick. Peel off the top sheet and invert the dough into the tart tin. Remove the bottom sheet. Ease the dough into the tin. Prick with a fork. Chill for 1 hour. Preheat the oven to 180°C/350°F/Gas 4.

3 Line the tart with foil and fill with baking beans. Bake blind for 5 minutes. Remove the foil and bake for 5 minutes, until set. Cool. For the filling, bring the cream to the boil in a pan. Remove from the heat, stir in the chocolate until smooth, then stir in the butter and brandy. Strain into the tart shell.

4 Spoon the melted white or milk chocolate into a paper piping bag and cut off the tip. Drop rounds of chocolate over the top and use a skewer to draw a point through the chocolate for a marbled effect. Chill for 3 hours, until set.

Nutritional information: Energy 474kcal/1969kJ; Protein 3.7g; Carbohydrate 32.5g, of which sugars 24.6g; Fat 36.8g, of which saturates 22.6g; Cholesterol 88mg; Calcium 48mg; Fibre 1.4g; Sodium 117mg.

Chilled chocolate and date slice

This delightfully crunchy dessert is delicious on its own, but it's also very good served with cream, or try it with fresh orange segments for something different.

SERVES 6–8

115g/4oz/¹/₂ cup unsalted (sweet) butter, melted
225g/8oz ginger nut biscuits (gingersnaps), finely crushed
50g/2oz/²/₃ cup stale sponge cake crumbs
75ml/5 tbsp orange juice

115g/4oz/²/₃ cup pitted dates
25g/1oz/¹/₄ cup finely chopped nuts
175g/6oz dark (bittersweet) chocolate
300ml/¹/₂ pint/1¹/₄ cups whipping cream
grated chocolate and icing (confectioners') sugar, to decorate

1 Mix the butter and ginger biscuit crumbs in a bowl, then press the mixture on to the sides and base of an 18cm/7in loose-based flan tin (pan). Chill while making the filling.

2 Put the sponge cake crumbs into a bowl. Pour over 60ml/4 tbsp of the orange juice, stir well and leave to soak. Put the dates in a pan and add the remaining orange juice. Warm the mixture over a low heat. Mash the warm dates thoroughly and stir in the cake crumbs, with the finely chopped nuts.

3 Mix the chocolate with 60ml/4 tbsp of the cream in a heatproof bowl. Place the bowl over a pan of barely simmering water and stir occasionally until melted. In a separate bowl, whip the rest of the cream to soft peaks, then fold in the melted chocolate.

4 Add the cooled date mixture to the cream and chocolate and mix thoroughly. Pour into the crumb crust and level the mixture. Chill until just set, then mark the tart into portions, using a knife dipped in hot water. Chill until firm. Sprinkle over the grated chocolate and dust with icing sugar.

Nutritional information: Energy 575kcal/2394kJ; Protein 5.1g; Carbohydrate 51.3g, of which sugars 37.5g; Fat 40.2g, of which saturates 22.8g; Cholesterol 78mg; Calcium 87mg; Fibre 1.8g; Sodium 214mg.

Chocolate vanilla timbales

These timbales are elegant enough for any special occasion, but are deceptively low in calories – ideal when you've been over-indulging a bit, but still feel like a treat.

SERVES 6

350ml/12fl oz/1¹/₂ cups semi-skimmed (low-fat) milk
30ml/2 tbsp unsweetened cocoa powder
2 eggs, separated
10ml/2 tsp vanilla extract
45ml/3 tbsp granulated sweetener
15ml/1 tbsp/1 sachet powdered gelatine
45ml/3 tbsp hot water
extra cocoa powder, to decorate

FOR THE SAUCE
115g/4oz/¹/₂ cup light Greek (US strained plain) yogurt
25ml/1¹/₂ tbsp vanilla extract

1 Place the milk and cocoa powder in a pan and stir until the milk is boiling. Beat the egg yolks with the vanilla and sweetener in a bowl, until the mixture is pale and smooth. Gradually pour in the chocolate milk, beating well.

2 Return the mixture to the pan and stir constantly over a gentle heat, without boiling, until it is slightly thickened and smooth.

3 Remove the pan from the heat. Add the gelatine to the hot water and stir until it is completely dissolved, then quickly stir it into the milk mixture. Put this mixture aside and allow it to cool until almost setting.

4 Whisk the egg whites until they hold soft peaks. Fold the egg whites quickly into the milk mixture. Spoon the timbale mixture into six individual moulds and chill them until set.

5 To serve, run a knife around the edge, dip the moulds quickly into hot water and turn out. Dust with cocoa. For the sauce, stir together the yogurt and vanilla and serve in a separate dish.

Nutritional information: Energy 89kcal/372kJ; Protein 6.2g; Carbohydrate 3.7g, of which sugars 3.1g; Fat 5.9g, of which saturates 2.8g; Cholesterol 67mg; Calcium 115mg; Fibre 0.6g; Sodium 110mg.

Chocolate and chestnut pots

These rich little pots are the perfect ending for a dinner party. For the very best flavour, remove them from the refrigerator about 30 minutes before serving, to allow them to "ripen".

SERVES 6

250g/9oz plain (semisweet) chocolate
60ml/4 tbsp Madeira
25g/1oz/2 tbsp butter, diced
2 eggs, separated
225g/8oz/1 cup unsweetened chestnut
   purée
crème fraîche or whipped double (heavy)
   cream, to serve

1 Make a few chocolate curls for decoration, then break the rest of the chocolate into squares and melt it with the Madeira in a pan over a gentle heat. Remove from the heat and add the butter, a few pieces at a time, stirring until melted and smooth.

2 Beat the egg yolks quickly into the mixture, then beat in the chestnut purée, mixing until smooth.

3 Whisk the egg whites in a clean, grease-free bowl until stiff. Stir about 15ml/1 tbsp of the whites into the chestnut mixture to lighten it, then fold in the rest evenly.

4 Spoon the mixture into six small ramekin dishes and chill until set. Serve the pots topped with a generous spoonful of crème fraîche or whipped cream. Decorate with the plain chocolate curls.

Nutritional information: Energy 348kcal/1455kJ; Protein 5g; Carbohydrate 41.4g, of which sugars 29.9g; Fat 18g, of which saturates 9.9g; Cholesterol 75mg; Calcium 42mg; Fibre 2.6g; Sodium 56mg.

Chocolate profiteroles

These little golden puffs filled with simple vanilla ice cream cannot fail to impress. A timeless classic, chocolate profiteroles will always add a special touch to a party.

SERVES 4–6

110g/3³⁄₄oz/scant 1 cup plain (all-
  purpose) flour
1.5ml/¹⁄₄ tsp salt
pinch of freshly grated nutmeg
175ml/6fl oz/³⁄₄ cup water
75g/3oz/6 tbsp unsalted (sweet) butter,
  cut into pieces
3 eggs
750ml/1¹⁄₄ pints/3 cups vanilla ice cream

FOR THE CHOCOLATE SAUCE

275g/10oz plain (semisweet) chocolate,
  chopped into small pieces
120ml/4fl oz/¹⁄₂ cup warm water

1 Preheat the oven to 200°C/400°F/Gas 6. Grease a baking sheet. Sift the flour, salt and nutmeg on to a sheet of baking parchment or foil. For the sauce, melt the chocolate and water in a heatproof bowl set over a pan of simmering water. Stir until smooth. Keep warm.

2 Put the water and butter in a pan and bring to the boil. Remove from the heat and add the dry ingredients all at once. Beat with a wooden spoon for 1 minute until blended and the mixture starts to pull away from the pan. Set over a low heat and cook for 2 minutes, beating. Remove from the heat.

3 Beat 1 egg in a bowl and set aside. Add the remaining eggs, one at a time, to the flour mix, beating after each addition. Beat in just enough of the beaten egg to make a smooth, shiny dough. It should pull away and fall slowly when dropped from a spoon.

4 Using a tablespoon, ease the dough in 12 mounds on to the prepared baking sheet. Bake for 25–30 minutes, until the puffs are golden brown. Remove the puffs from the oven and cut a small slit in the side of each of them to release the steam. Return the puffs to the oven, turn off the heat and leave to dry out, with the door open.

5 Remove the ice cream from the freezer and allow it to soften for about 10 minutes. Split the profiteroles in half and put a small scoop of ice cream in each. Serve with the sauce.

Nutritional information: Energy 647kcal/2707kJ; Protein 11.7g; Carbohydrate 68.2g, of which sugars 52.4g; Fat 36.9g, of which saturates 22.7g; Cholesterol 155mg; Calcium 182mg; Fibre 1.7g; Sodium 189mg.

Bitter chocolate mousse

An intense chocolate taste with a hint of alcohol, and a divinely smooth, creamy texture, make this sophisticated dessert ideal for a special dinner party.

SERVES 8

225g/8oz plain (semisweet) chocolate,
   chopped into small pieces
60ml/4 tbsp water
30ml/2 tbsp orange liqueur or brandy
25g/1oz/2 tbsp unsalted (sweet) butter,
   cut into small pieces
4 eggs, separated

90ml/6 tbsp whipping cream
1.5ml/¼ tsp cream of tartar
45ml/3 tbsp caster (superfine) sugar
crème fraîche and chocolate curls,
   to decorate

1 Melt the chocolate with the water in a heatproof bowl over a pan of barely simmering water, stirring until smooth. Off the heat, whisk in the liqueur or brandy and butter.

2 With a hand-held electric mixer, beat the egg yolks for 2–3 minutes until thick and creamy, then slowly beat into the melted chocolate until well blended. Set aside.

3 Whip the cream until soft peaks form and stir a spoonful into the chocolate mixture to lighten it. Fold in the remaining cream.

4 In a clean, grease-free bowl, beat the egg whites slowly until frothy. Add the cream of tartar, increase the speed and continue beating until they form soft peaks. Gradually sprinkle over the sugar and continue beating until the whites are stiff and glossy.

5 Using a rubber spatula or large metal spoon, stir a quarter of the egg whites into the chocolate mixture, then gently fold in the remaining whites, cutting down to the bottom, along the sides and up to the top in a semicircular motion until they are just combined. Gently spoon into eight individual dishes. Chill for at least 2 hours or until set.

6 Spoon a little crème fraîche over each mousse and decorate with the chocolate curls.

Nutritional information: Energy 236kcal/988kJ; Protein 5.5g; Carbohydrate 25.7g, of which sugars 25.4g; Fat 12.2g, of which saturates 6.2g; Cholesterol 121mg; Calcium 31mg; Fibre 0.8g; Sodium 46mg.

White chocolate mousse

Happy endings are assured when slices of creamy white chocolate mousse are served with a divine dark chocolate sauce laced with rum.

SERVES 6–8

200g/7oz white chocolate,
   broken into squares
2 eggs, separated
60ml/4 tbsp caster (superfine) sugar
300ml/1/2 pint/11/4 cups double
   (heavy) cream
1 sachet powdered gelatine
150ml/5fl oz/2/3 cup Greek (US strained
   plain) yogurt
10ml/2 tsp vanilla extract

FOR THE SAUCE

50g/2oz plain (semisweet) chocolate,
   broken into squares
30ml/2 tbsp dark rum
60ml/4 tbsp single (light) cream

1 Line a 1-litre/13/4-pint/4-cup loaf tin (pan) with baking parchment. Melt the white chocolate in a heatproof bowl over simmering water, then remove from the heat.

2 Whisk the egg yolks and sugar in a bowl until pale and thick, then beat in the melted chocolate.

3 Heat the cream in a small pan until almost boiling, then remove from the heat. Sprinkle the powdered gelatine over, stirring until completely dissolved. Pour on to the chocolate mixture, whisking vigorously until smooth.

4 Whisk the yogurt and vanilla extract into the mixture. In a clean, grease-free bowl, whisk the egg whites until stiff, then fold them into the mixture. Turn into the prepared loaf tin, level the surface and chill until set.

5 Make the sauce. Melt the chocolate with the rum and cream in a heatproof bowl over simmering water, stirring occasionally, then leave to cool completely.

6 When the mousse is set, remove from the tin. Serve in slices with the cooled chocolate sauce.

Nutritional information: Energy 433kcal/1796kJ; Protein 6g; Carbohydrate 25g, of which sugars 24.9g; Fat 34.4g, of which saturates 20.5g; Cholesterol 103mg; Calcium 133mg; Fibre 0.2g; Sodium 69mg.

Italian chocolate ricotta pie

This glorious pie makes a perfect treat for a spontaneous al fresco picnic – leave it in the tin to pack it. Serve with whipped cream to make it even more special.

SERVES 6

225g/8oz/2 cups plain (all-purpose) flour
30ml/2 tbsp unsweetened cocoa powder
60ml/4 tbsp caster (superfine) sugar
115g/4oz/¹/₂ cup unsalted
   (sweet) butter
60ml/4 tbsp dry sherry
whipped cream, to serve

FOR THE FILLING

2 egg yolks
115g/4oz/¹/₂ cup caster
   (superfine) sugar
500g/1¹/₄lb/2¹/₂ cups ricotta cheese
finely grated rind of 1 lemon
90ml/6 tbsp dark (bittersweet)
   chocolate chips
75ml/5 tbsp mixed chopped
   (candied) peel
45ml/3 tbsp chopped angelica

1 Preheat the oven to 200°C/400°F/ Gas 6. Sift the flour and cocoa into a bowl, then stir in the sugar. Rub in the butter until the mixture resembles breadcrumbs. Work in the sherry, with your fingertips, until the mixture binds to a firm dough.

2 Roll out three-quarters of the pastry and line a 24cm/9¹/₂in loose-based flan tin (pan).

3 Beat the egg yolks and sugar in a bowl, then beat in the ricotta. Stir in the lemon rind, chocolate chips, mixed peel and angelica.

4 Spoon the ricotta mixture into the pastry case and level the surface.

5 Roll out the remaining pastry and cut into strips, then arrange these in a lattice over the pie.

6 Bake the pie for 15 minutes, then lower the oven temperature to 180°C/350°F/Gas 4 and cook for a further 30–35 minutes, or until the pie is golden brown and firm to the touch.

7 Allow the pie to cool in the tin before serving with whipped cream.

Nutritional information: Energy 701kcal/2938kJ; Protein 14.2g; Carbohydrate 83.4g, of which sugars 54.1g; Fat 35.6g, of which saturates 21.3g; Cholesterol 144mg; Calcium 115mg; Fibre 3g; Sodium 223mg.

Chocolate hazelnut galettes

Fromage frais makes a wonderful creamy filling for these elegant galettes, but if you can't find any, you could use cream cheese or mascarpone instead.

SERVES 4

175g/6oz plain (semisweet) chocolate,
   broken into squares
45ml/3 tbsp single (light) cream
30ml/2 tbsp flaked (sliced) hazelnuts
115g/4oz white chocolate, broken
   into squares

175g/6oz/¾ cup fromage frais
15ml/1 tbsp dry sherry
60ml/4 tbsp finely chopped
   hazelnuts, toasted
physalis (Cape gooseberries), dipped in
   white chocolate, to decorate

1 Melt the plain chocolate in a heatproof bowl over simmering water, then remove from the heat and stir in the cream.

2 Draw 12 x 7.5cm/3in circles on sheets of baking parchment. Turn the paper over and spread the plain chocolate over each marked circle, covering in a thin, even layer. Scatter flaked hazelnuts over four of the circles, then leave until set.

3 Melt the white chocolate in a heatproof bowl over simmering water, then stir in the fromage frais and dry sherry. Fold in the chopped, toasted hazelnuts. Leave to cool until the mixture holds its shape.

4 Remove the plain chocolate rounds carefully from the paper and sandwich them together in stacks of three, spooning the white chocolate hazelnut cream between each layer and using the hazelnut-covered rounds on top. Chill before serving.

5 To serve, place the galettes on individual plates and decorate with chocolate-dipped physalis.

Nutritional information: Energy 597kcal/2489kJ; Protein 10.7g; Carbohydrate 48.1g, of which sugars 47.2g; Fat 41.1g, of which saturates 17.5g; Cholesterol 13mg; Calcium 182mg; Fibre 2.6g; Sodium 55mg.

Mango and chocolate crème brûlée

Pure luxury – exotic fruit in a honeyed chocolate custard, topped with a crunchy coating of caramelized sugar. Don't forget to chill it twice!

SERVES 6

2 ripe mangoes
300ml/¹⁄₂ pint/1¹⁄₄ cups double (heavy) cream
300ml/¹⁄₂ pint/1¹⁄₄ cups crème fraîche
1 vanilla pod (bean)
115g/4oz dark (bittersweet) chocolate, broken into squares
4 egg yolks
15ml/1 tbsp clear honey
90ml/6 tbsp demerara (raw) sugar

1 Halve, stone (pit) and peel the mangoes. Chop the flesh and divide it among six individual flameproof dishes set on a baking sheet.

2 Mix the double cream and crème fraîche in a large heatproof bowl and add the vanilla pod. Place the bowl over a pan of simmering water and stir for 10 minutes. Do not let the bowl touch the water or the cream may overheat.

3 Remove the vanilla pod and stir in the chocolate, a few pieces at a time, until melted. When the mixture is completely smooth, remove the bowl, but leave the pan of water over the heat.

4 Whisk the egg yolks and honey in a second heatproof bowl, then gradually pour in the chocolate cream, whisking constantly. Place over the pan of simmering water and stir constantly until the chocolate custard thickens enough to coat the back of a wooden spoon. Remove from the heat and spoon the custard over the mangoes. Cool, then chill until set.

5 Preheat the grill (broiler) to high. Sprinkle 15ml/1 tbsp demerara sugar over each dessert and spray lightly with a little water. Grill (broil) briefly, as close to the heat as possible, until the sugar melts and caramelizes. Chill again before serving.

Nutritional information: Energy 670kcal/2782kJ; Protein 5.2g; Carbohydrate 38.9g, of which sugars 38.4g; Fat 56g, of which saturates 34.6g; Cholesterol 261mg; Calcium 90mg; Fibre 1.8g; Sodium 31mg.

Chocolate mandarin trifle

Everyone likes trifle, which makes it the perfect dish to serve at a party. The mandarin slices used here provide a sharp citrus contrast to the creamy chocolate custard.

SERVES 6–8

4 trifle sponges
14 amaretti
60ml/4 tbsp Amaretto di Sarone
8 mandarin oranges

FOR THE CUSTARD
200g/7oz plain (semisweet) chocolate,
**   broken into squares**
30ml/2 tbsp cornflour (cornstarch)
30ml/2 tbsp caster (superfine) sugar
2 egg yolks
200ml/7fl oz/scant 1 cup milk
250g/9oz/generous 1 cup mascarpone

FOR THE TOPPING
250g/9oz/generous 1 cup fromage frais
**   or mascarpone**
chocolate shapes
mandarin slices

1 Break up the trifle sponges and place them in a large glass serving dish. Crumble the amaretti over and then sprinkle with the Amaretto di Sarone.

2 Squeeze the juice from two mandarins and sprinkle into the dish. Segment the rest and put in the dish.

3 Make the custard. Melt the chocolate in a heatproof bowl over simmering water. In a separate bowl, mix the cornflour, sugar and egg yolks to a paste.

4 Heat the milk in a small pan until almost boiling, then pour into the egg yolk mixture, stirring constantly. Return to the clean pan and stir over a low heat until the custard has thickened slightly and is smooth.

5 Stir in the mascarpone until melted, then add the melted chocolate, mixing it evenly. Spread evenly over the trifle, cool, then chill until set.

6 Spread the fromage frais or mascarpone over the custard, then decorate with chocolate shapes and mandarin slices before serving.

Nutritional information: Energy 569kcal/2394kJ; Protein 12.5g; Carbohydrate 80.3g, of which sugars 61.3g; Fat 23.1g, of which saturates 12.8g; Cholesterol 135mg; Calcium 162mg; Fibre 2.9g; Sodium 115mg.

Chocolate cones with apricot sauce

These dark chocolate cones can be made, filled and arranged with the sauce on plates before you start your meal, then chilled ready to serve.

SERVES 6

250g/9oz dark (bittersweet) chocolate, broken into squares
350g/12oz/1½ cups ricotta cheese
45ml/3 tbsp double (heavy) cream
30ml/2 tbsp brandy
30ml/2 tbsp icing (confectioners') sugar
finely grated rind of 1 lemon
strips of lemon rind, to decorate

FOR THE SAUCE

175g/6oz/²/³ cup apricot jam
45ml/3 tbsp lemon juice

1 Cut 12 x 10cm/4in double thickness rounds from baking parchment and shape each into a cone. Secure with masking tape.

2 Melt the chocolate in a heatproof bowl over simmering water, cool slightly, then spoon a little into each cone, swirling and brushing it to coat the paper in an even layer.

3 Stand each cone point downwards in a cup or glass, to hold it straight. Leave in a cool place until the cones are completely set.

4 Make the sauce. Combine the apricot jam and lemon juice in a small pan. Melt over a gentle heat, then cool.

5 Beat the ricotta, cream, brandy and icing sugar in a bowl. Stir in the lemon rind. Spoon or pipe the ricotta mixture into the cones, then carefully peel off the paper.

6 Serve the cones in pairs on individual plates, sprinkled with lemon rind and surrounded with the cooled apricot sauce.

Nutritional information: Energy 461kcal/1932kJ; Protein 7.8g; Carbohydrate 53.8g, of which sugars 53.4g; Fat 24.2g, of which saturates 14.8g; Cholesterol 37mg; Calcium 24mg; Fibre 1g; Sodium 13mg.

Chocolate fudge sundaes

This family favourite can't fail to put a smile on children's faces, but leave out the liqueur if you're making it for them. Adults will appreciate the more sophisticated version.

SERVES 4

4 scoops each vanilla and coffee
   ice cream
2 small ripe bananas, peeled and
   thinly sliced
whipped cream and toasted flaked
   (sliced) almonds, to decorate

FOR THE SAUCE

50g/2oz/¹⁄₃ cup soft light brown sugar
120ml/4fl oz/¹⁄₂ cup golden (light
   corn) syrup
45ml/3 tbsp strong black coffee
5ml/1 tsp ground cinnamon
150g/5oz plain (semisweet) chocolate,
   chopped into small pieces
75ml/3fl oz/5 tbsp whipping cream
45ml/3 tbsp coffee-flavoured
   liqueur (optional)

1 Make the sauce. Place the sugar, syrup, coffee and cinnamon in a pan. Bring to the boil, then boil for 5 minutes, stirring constantly.

2 Turn off the heat and stir in the chocolate. When the chocolate has melted and the mixture is smooth, stir in the cream and the liqueur, if using.

3 Leave the sauce to cool slightly. If made ahead, reheat the sauce gently until just warm.

4 Fill four glasses with a scoop each of vanilla and coffee ice cream. Sprinkle the sliced bananas over the ice cream.

5 Carefully pour the warm fudge sauce over the top of the bananas, then top each of the sundaes with a generous swirl of whipped cream.

6 Sprinkle the top of the each sundae with toasted almonds, then serve immediately.

Nutritional information: Energy 595kcal/2498kJ; Protein 6.3g; Carbohydrate 88.1g, of which sugars 85.3g; Fat 26.5g, of which saturates 14.1g; Cholesterol 26mg; Calcium 139mg; Fibre 1.8g; Sodium 144mg.

White chocolate raspberry ripple ice cream

There is nothing more delicious than homemade ice cream. The combination of creamy white chocolate and sweet raspberry sauce makes this dessert simply divine.

SERVES 4

250ml/8fl oz/1 cup milk
475ml/16fl oz/2 cups whipping cream
7 egg yolks
30ml/2 tbsp sugar
225g/8oz white chocolate, chopped into
   small pieces
5ml/1 tsp vanilla extract
mint sprigs, to decorate

**FOR THE RASPBERRY
RIPPLE SAUCE**

275g/10oz packet frozen raspberries in
   light syrup or 275g/10oz jar reduced-
   sugar raspberry preserve
10ml/2 tsp golden (light corn) syrup
15ml/1 tbsp lemon juice
15ml/1 tbsp cornflour (cornstarch) mixed
   to a paste with 15ml/1 tbsp water

1 Prepare the sauce. Press the raspberries and their syrup through a sieve (strainer) into a pan. Add the golden syrup, lemon juice and cornflour mixture. (If using preserve, omit cornflour, but add the water.) Bring to the boil, stirring often, then simmer for 1–2 minutes. Pour into a bowl and cool, then chill.

2 In a pan, combine the milk and 250ml/8fl oz/1 cup of the cream and bring to the boil. In a bowl, beat the yolks and sugar with a hand-held mixer for 2–3 minutes until thick and creamy. Gradually pour the hot milk mixture over the yolks and return to the pan. Cook over a medium heat until the custard coats the back of a wooden spoon, stirring constantly.

3 Remove the pan from the heat and stir in the white chocolate until melted and smooth. Pour the remaining cream into a large bowl. Strain in the hot custard, mix well, then stir in the vanilla extract. Cool, then transfer the custard to an ice cream maker and freeze it according to the manufacturer's instructions.

4 When the mixture is frozen, but still soft, transfer one-third of the ice cream to a freezerproof bowl. Set half the raspberry sauce aside. Spoon a third of the remainder over the ice cream. Cover with another third of the ice cream and more sauce. Repeat. With a knife or spoon, lightly marble the mixture. Cover and freeze. Allow the ice cream to soften for 15 minutes before serving with the remaining raspberry sauce, decorated with the mint.

Nutritional information: Energy 4045kcal/16819kJ; Protein 58.3g; Carbohydrate 286.5g, of which sugars 272.7g; Fat 304g, of which saturates 174.9g; Cholesterol 1925mg; Calcium 1408mg; Fibre 4.1g; Sodium 638mg.

Rocky road ice cream

For chills and thrills, there's nothing to beat this classic, sweet ice cream packed with contrasting textures and flavours. Sure to be a favourite at birthday parties.

SERVES 6

115g/4oz plain (semisweet) chocolate, broken into squares
150ml/¼ pint/⅔ cup milk
300ml/½ pint/1¼ cups double (heavy) cream
115g/4oz/1½ cups marshmallows, chopped
50g/2oz/½ cup glacé (candied) cherries, chopped
50g/2oz/½ cup crumbled shortbread biscuits
30ml/2 tbsp chopped walnuts

1 Melt the chocolate in the milk in a pan over a gentle heat, stirring from time to time. Leave to cool completely.

2 Whip the double cream in a bowl until it just holds its shape. Beat in the chocolate mixture.

3 Turn the mixture into an ice cream maker and churn until thick and almost frozen. Alternatively, pour into a container suitable for use in the freezer, freeze until ice crystals form around the edges, then whisk until smooth.

4 Stir the marshmallows, cherries, crushed biscuits and nuts into the iced mixture, then return to the freezer container and freeze until firm.

5 Allow the ice cream to soften at room temperature for 15–20 minutes before serving in scoops.

Nutritional information: Energy 545kcal/2271kJ; Protein 4.7g; Carbohydrate 48.3g, of which sugars 40.6g; Fat 38.4g, of which saturates 22g; Cholesterol 77mg; Calcium 85mg; Fibre 1g; Sodium 57mg.

Chocolate sorbet

Using only the simplest of ingredients, this mouthwatering chocolate-flavoured sorbet looks and tastes delicious and will round off any meal perfectly.

SERVES 6

150g/5oz dark (bittersweet)
   chocolate, chopped
115g/4oz plain (semisweet)
   chocolate, grated
225g/8oz/1¼ cups caster
   (superfine) sugar
475ml/16fl oz/2 cups water
chocolate curls, to decorate

1 Put all the chocolate in a food processor, fitted with the metal blade, and process for 20–30 seconds until finely chopped.

2 Bring the sugar and water to the boil, over a medium heat, stirring until the sugar dissolves. Boil for about 2 minutes, then remove the pan from the heat.

3 With the machine running, pour the hot syrup over the chocolate in the food processor. Keep the machine running for 1–2 minutes until the chocolate is completely melted and the mixture is smooth, scraping down the bowl once.

4 Strain the chocolate mixture into a bowl. Leave to cool, then chill, stirring occasionally. Freeze the mixture in an ice cream maker. Alternatively, pour into a container suitable for use in the freezer, freeze until slushy, whisk until smooth, then freeze again. Whisk for a second time before the mixture hardens completely. Allow the sorbet to soften for 5–10 minutes at room temperature and serve in scoops, decorated with chocolate curls.

Nutritional information: Energy 301kcal/1266kJ; Protein 2.3g; Carbohydrate 48.1g, of which sugars 47.7g; Fat 12.4g, of which saturates 7.4g; Cholesterol 3mg; Calcium 25mg; Fibre 1.1g; Sodium 4mg.

Chocolate mint ice cream pie

This simple pie is incredibly easy to make. The crispy cereal base and mint-chocolate-chip ice cream are sure to make this a big hit with children.

SERVES 8

75g/3 oz plain (semisweet)
   chocolate chips
40g/1¹/₂oz butter or margarine
50g/2oz crisped rice cereal
1 litre/1³/₄ pints/4 cups
   mint-chocolate-chip ice cream
chocolate curls, to decorate

1 Line a 23cm/9in pie tin (pan) with foil. Place a round of baking parchment over the foil in the bottom of the tin.

2 In a heatproof bowl, set over a pan of simmering water, melt the chocolate chips with the butter or margarine. Remove the bowl from the heat and gently stir in the cereal, a little at a time.

3 Press the chocolate-cereal mixture evenly over the base and up the sides of the prepared tin, forming a 1cm/¹/₂in rim. Chill until completely hard.

4 Carefully remove the cereal base from the tin and peel off the foil and paper. Return the base to the pie tin.

5 Remove the ice cream from the freezer and allow it to soften for 10 minutes. Spread the ice cream in the cereal case. Freeze until firm. Sprinkle the chocolate curls over the ice cream just before serving.

Nutritional information: Energy 378kcal/1573kJ; Protein 6.1g; Carbohydrate 32g, of which sugars 27.2g; Fat 25.9g, of which saturates 15.5g; Cholesterol 11mg; Calcium 183mg; Fibre 0.2g; Sodium 108mg.

Mocha velvet cream pots

These gorgeous little treats are great to serve at dinner parties as they can be prepared the day before and stored in the refrigerator until you are ready for them.

SERVES 8

15ml/1 tbsp instant coffee powder
475ml/16fl oz/2 cups milk
75g/3oz/6 tbsp caster (superfine) sugar
225g/8oz plain (semisweet) chocolate,
**   chopped into small pieces**
10ml/2 tsp vanilla extract
30ml/2 tbsp coffee liqueur (optional)
7 egg yolks
whipped cream and crystallized mimosa
**   balls, to decorate**

1 Preheat the oven to 160°C/325°F/Gas 3. Place eight 120ml/4fl oz/$^1/_2$ cup ramekins in a roasting pan. Put the coffee into a pan. Stir in the milk, add the sugar and bring to the boil, stirring, until the coffee and the sugar have dissolved.

2 Remove from the heat and add the chocolate. Stir until it has melted and the sauce is smooth. Stir in the vanilla extract and coffee liqueur, if using.

3 In a bowl, whisk the egg yolks to blend them lightly. Slowly whisk in the chocolate mixture until well mixed, then strain the mixture into a jug (pitcher) and divide equally among the ramekins. Pour enough boiling water into the roasting pan to come halfway up the sides of the ramekins.

4 Bake for 30–35 minutes, until the custard is just set and a knife inserted into the custard comes out clean. Remove from the roasting pan and cool. Place on a baking sheet, cover and chill. Decorate with whipped cream and crystallized mimosa balls, before serving.

Nutritional information: Energy 261kcal/1095kJ; Protein 6g; Carbohydrate 30.5g, of which sugars 30.2g; Fat 13.7g, of which saturates 6.7g; Cholesterol 182mg; Calcium 106mg; Fibre 0.7g; Sodium 36mg.

Chocolate sorbet with red fruits

The chill that thrills – that's chocolate sorbet. For a really fine texture, it helps to have an ice cream maker, which churns the mixture as it freezes, but you can make it by hand quite easily.

SERVES 6

475ml/16fl oz/2 cups water
45ml/3 tbsp clear honey
115g/4oz/$^{1}/_{2}$ cup caster
   (superfine) sugar
75g/3oz/$^{3}/_{4}$ cup unsweetened
   cocoa powder

50g/2oz dark (bittersweet) chocolate,
   broken into squares
400g/14oz soft red fruits,
   such as raspberries, redcurrants
   or strawberries, to decorate

1 Place the water, honey, sugar and cocoa in a large pan. Heat gently, stirring occasionally, until the sugar has completely dissolved.

2 Remove the pan from the heat, add the chocolate and stir until it has melted. Leave until cool.

3 Turn into an ice cream maker and churn until frozen. Alternatively, pour into a container suitable for use in the freezer, freeze until slushy, whisk until smooth, then freeze again. Whisk for a second time before the mixture hardens completely.

4 Remove from the freezer 10–15 minutes before serving, so that the sorbet softens slightly. Serve in scoops, with the soft fruits.

Nutritional information: Energy 179kcal/758kJ; Protein 3.8g; Carbohydrate 31.2g, of which sugars 29.7g; Fat 5.3g, of which saturates 3.1g; Cholesterol 1mg; Calcium 44mg; Fibre 3.4g; Sodium 123mg.

Sweets and drinks

Chocolate truffles and nutty fudge are

simple and rewarding to make, and,

packed into pretty boxes or jars, they

make wonderful gifts. If you prefer liquid

chocolate, at the end of the day you can

sink into a comfy armchair with a

warming glass of Irish Chocolate Velvet

or Mexican Hot Chocolate.

Malt whisky truffles

These tempting truffles make perfect presents – if you can part with them.

MAKES 25–30

200g/7oz dark (bittersweet) chocolate,
   broken into squares
150ml/¼ pint/⅔ cup double (heavy) cream
45ml/3 tbsp malt whisky
115g/4oz/1 cup icing (confectioners') sugar
unsweetened cocoa powder, for coating

1 Melt the chocolate in a heatproof bowl over simmering water, then cool slightly.

2 Whip the cream with the whisky in a bowl until thick enough to hold its shape.

3 Stir in the chocolate and icing sugar, mixing evenly, then leave until firm enough to handle.

4 Dust your hands with cocoa and shape the mixture into bitesize balls. Coat in cocoa powder and pack into pretty cases or boxes. Store in the refrigerator for up to 3–4 days if necessary.

Nutritional information: Energy 77kcal/323kJ; Protein 0.4g; Carbohydrate 8.3g, of which sugars 8.3g; Fat 4.6g, of which saturates 2.8g; Cholesterol 7mg; Calcium 7mg; Fibre 0.2g; Sodium 2mg.

Fondant hearts

Pipe your loved one's initials on to these luscious love tokens for a special touch.

MAKES ABOUT 50

60ml/4 tbsp liquid glucose
50g/2oz dark (bittersweet) chocolate, broken into squares
50g/2oz white chocolate, broken into squares
1 egg white, lightly beaten, plus extra for brushing
450g/1lb/3½ cups icing (confectioners') sugar, sifted
melted dark and white chocolate, to decorate

1 Divide the glucose between two heatproof bowls. Place each bowl over simmering water and heat the glucose gently, then add the dark chocolate to one bowl and the white chocolate to the other. Leave until the chocolate has completely melted.

2 Remove both bowls from the heat and cool slightly. Add half the egg white to each bowl, then divide the icing sugar between them, mixing to combine well.

3 Knead each mixture separately with your hands until it is smooth and pliable. On a surface lightly dusted with icing sugar, roll out both mixtures separately to a thickness of about 3mm/⅛in.

4 Brush the surface of the dark chocolate fondant with egg white and place the white chocolate fondant on top. Roll the surface lightly with a rolling pin to press the pieces together.

5 Using a small heart-shaped cutter, stamp out about 50 hearts from the fondant. Drizzle melted chocolate over each heart to decorate and leave until firm.

Nutritional information: Energy 50kcal/212kJ; Protein 0.2g; Carbohydrate 11.6g, of which sugars 11.1g; Fat 0.6g, of which saturates 0.4g; Cholesterol 0mg; Calcium 8mg; Fibre 0g; Sodium 5mg.

Chocolate almond torrone

Triangles of smooth dark chocolate, laced with chopped almonds, encased in delicious white chocolate. Serve this Italian speciality in thin slices.

MAKES ABOUT 20 SLICES

115g/4oz dark (bittersweet) chocolate,
broken into squares
50g/2oz/4 tbsp unsalted (sweet) butter
1 egg white
115g/4oz/1/2 cup caster (superfine)
sugar
50g/2oz/1/2 cup ground almonds
75g/3oz/11/2 cups chopped
toasted almonds
75ml/5 tbsp chopped candied peel

FOR THE COATING

175g/6oz white chocolate, broken
into squares
25g/1oz/2 tbsp unsalted (sweet) butter
115g/4oz/1 cup flaked (sliced)
almonds, toasted

1 Melt the chocolate with the butter in a heatproof bowl over barely simmering water until smooth.

2 In a clean, grease-free bowl, whisk the egg white with the sugar until stiff. Gradually beat in the melted chocolate, then stir in the ground almonds, chopped toasted almonds and peel. Turn the mixture on to a large sheet of baking parchment and shape into a thick roll.

3 As the mixture cools, use the paper to press the roll firmly into a triangular shape. Twist the paper over the triangular roll and chill until completely set.

4 Make the coating. Melt the white chocolate with the butter in a heatproof bowl over simmering water. Unwrap the chocolate roll and spread the white chocolate quickly over the surface. Press the almonds in a thin even coating over the chocolate, working quickly before the chocolate sets. Chill again until firm, then cut the torrone into fairly thin slices to serve.

Nutritional information: Energy 186kcal/775kJ; Protein 3.7g; Carbohydrate 11.8g, of which sugars 11.4g; Fat 14.1g, of which saturates 5.1g; Cholesterol 8mg; Calcium 60mg; Fibre 1.2g; Sodium 48mg.

Chocolate Christmas cups

These adorable little cups are perfect for that extra-special treat to enjoy with a mid-afternoon cup of coffee or tea, and are an excellent way of using up leftover Christmas pudding.

MAKES ABOUT 35 CUPS

275g/10oz plain (semisweet) chocolate,
   chopped into small pieces
175g/6oz cold cooked Christmas pudding
75ml/2¹/₂fl oz/5 tbsp brandy or whisky
crystallized cranberries, to decorate

1 Melt the chocolate in a heatproof bowl over simmering water and use to coat the insides of about 35 sweet (candy) cases. Allow to set, then repeat, reheating the melted chocolate if necessary.

2 Leave the chocolate cups to cool and set. Reserve the remaining chocolate. Crumble the Christmas pudding into a small bowl, sprinkle with brandy or whisky and allow to stand for 30–40 minutes, until the liquid is absorbed.

3 Spoon a little of the pudding mixture into each cup, smoothing the top. Reheat the remaining chocolate and spoon over the top of each cup to cover the surface.

4 Leave to set, then peel off the cases. Decorate with crystallized cranberries.

Nutritional information: Energy 59kcal/249kJ; Protein 0.6g; Carbohydrate 7.5g, of which sugars 6.6g; Fat 2.7g, of which saturates 1.3g; Cholesterol 0mg; Calcium 7mg; Fibre 0.3g; Sodium 10mg.

Chocolate and cherry colettes

People always appreciate homemade gifts. For a sweet surprise for a friend or lover, pack these pretty little sweets in a decorative box.

MAKES 18–20

115g/4oz dark (bittersweet) chocolate,
    broken into squares
75g/3oz white or milk chocolate, broken
    into squares
25g/1oz/2 tbsp unsalted (sweet)
    butter, melted
15ml/1 tbsp Kirsch
60ml/4 tbsp double (heavy) cream
18–20 maraschino cherries or liqueur-
    soaked cherries
milk chocolate curls, to decorate

1 Melt the dark chocolate in a bowl over simmering water, then remove from the heat. Spoon into 18–20 foil sweet (candy) cases, spread evenly up the sides with a small brush, then leave in a cool place to set.

2 Melt the white or milk chocolate with the butter in a heatproof bowl set over a pan of simmering water. Remove from the heat and stir in the Kirsch, then the cream.

3 Leave the mixture until it is thick enough to hold its shape.

4 Place a cherry in each chocolate case. Spoon the chocolate cream mixture into a piping bag fitted with a small star nozzle and pipe over the cherries mounded in a swirl.

5 Top each colette with a chocolate curl and leave until set. Chill in the refrigerator until needed.

Nutritional information: Energy 163kcal/675kJ; Protein 0.7g; Carbohydrate 6.9g, of which sugars 6.8g; Fat 14.7g, of which saturates 9.2g; Cholesterol 31mg; Calcium 17mg; Fibre 0.2g; Sodium 82mg.

Cognac and ginger creams

Only you know the secret of these handsome hand-made chocolates: that the mysterious dark exterior conceals a glorious ginger and cognac cream filling.

MAKES 18–20

300g/11oz dark (bittersweet) chocolate, broken into squares
45ml/3 tbsp double (heavy) cream
30ml/2 tbsp cognac
15ml/1 tbsp stem ginger syrup
4 pieces preserved stem ginger, finely chopped
crystallized ginger, to decorate

1 Polish the insides of 18–20 chocolate moulds with cotton wool (cotton balls). Melt two-thirds of the chocolate in a heatproof bowl set over a pan of simmering water, then spoon a little into each mould. Reserve a little of the melted chocolate for sealing the creams.

2 Using a small brush, sweep the chocolate up the sides of the moulds to coat them evenly, then invert them on to a sheet of baking parchment and leave to set.

3 Melt the remaining chocolate, then stir in the cream, cognac, ginger syrup and stem ginger, mixing well. Spoon into the chocolate-lined moulds. Warm the reserved chocolate if necessary, then spoon a little into each mould to seal. Leave to stand in a cool place (not the refrigerator) until set.

4 To remove the chocolates from the moulds, gently press them out on to a cool surface. Decorate with small pieces of crystallized ginger.

Nutritional information: Energy 92kcal/383kJ; Protein 0.8g; Carbohydrate 10.2g, of which sugars 10g; Fat 5.4g, of which saturates 3.3g; Cholesterol 4mg; Calcium 6mg; Fibre 0.4g; Sodium 3mg.

Chocolate truffles

A time-honoured classic, truffles always add a sense of luxury to an occasion. For a different flavour, you could use your favourite liqueur instead of the brandy or whisky.

MAKES 20 LARGE OR 30 MEDIUM TRUFFLES

250ml/8fl oz/1 cup double (heavy) cream
275g/10oz dark (bittersweet) chocolate,
    chopped into pieces
40g/1¹/₂oz/3 tbsp unsalted (sweet)
    butter, cut into small pieces
45ml/3 tbsp brandy or whisky

TO COAT AND DECORATE

unsweetened cocoa powder,
    for dusting
finely chopped pistachio nuts and
    crystallized (candied) fruit, to decorate
400g/14oz dark (bittersweet) chocolate,
    for coating

1 Pour the cream into a pan. Bring to the boil over a medium heat. Remove from the heat and add the chocolate, all at once. Stir gently until melted. Stir in the butter until melted, then stir in the brandy or whisky liqueur. Strain into a bowl and cool to room temperature. Cover the mixture with clear film (plastic wrap) and chill for 4 hours or overnight.

2 Line a large baking sheet with baking parchment. Using a small ice cream scoop or tablespoon, scrape up the mixture into 20 large balls or 30 medium balls and place on the lined baking sheet. Dip the scoop or spoon in cold water from time to time, to prevent the mixture from sticking.

3 If dusting with cocoa powder, sift a thick layer of cocoa on to a dish or pie plate. Roll the truffles in the cocoa, rounding them between the palms of your hands. (Dust your hands with cocoa to prevent the truffles from sticking.) Do not worry if the truffles are not perfectly round as an irregular shape looks more homemade. Alternatively, roll the truffles in very finely chopped pistachios. Chill on the lined baking sheet until firm. Keep in the refrigerator for up to 10 days or freeze for up to 2 months.

4 If coating with chocolate, do not roll the truffles in cocoa or nuts, but freeze them for 1 hour. For perfect results, temper the chocolate (see page 189). Alternatively, simply melt it in a heatproof bowl over a pan of barely simmering water.

5 Using a fork, dip the truffles, one at a time, into the melted chocolate, allowing excess to drip off. Press a piece of crystallized fruit into each, if using. Place on a baking sheet, lined with baking parchment. If the chocolate begins to thicken, reheat it gently until smooth. Chill the truffles until set.

Nutritional information: Energy 101kcal/421kJ; Protein 0.6g; Carbohydrate 6g, of which sugars 5.9g; Fat 8.1g, of which saturates 5g; Cholesterol 15mg; Calcium 7mg; Fibre 0.2g; Sodium 10mg.

Rich chocolate pistachio fudge

Be sure to make a big batch of this meltingly rich chocolate fudge packed with pistachios – it won't last long! Try making it with almonds or walnuts, or a mixture of nuts and raisins.

MAKES 36 PIECES

250g/9oz/generous 1 cup sugar

375g/13oz can sweetened condensed milk

50g/2oz/4 tbsp unsalted (sweet) butter

5ml/1 tsp vanilla extract

115g/4oz plain dark chocolate, grated

75g/3oz/¾ cup pistachios

1 Grease a 19cm/7½in square cake tin (pan) and line with baking parchment. Mix the sugar, condensed milk and butter in a heavy pan. Heat gently, stirring occasionally, until the sugar has dissolved completely.

2 Bring the mixture to the boil, stirring occasionally, and boil until it registers 116°C/240°F on a sugar thermometer.

3 Remove the pan from the heat and beat in the vanilla extract, chocolate and nuts. Beat vigorously until the mixture is smooth and creamy.

4 Pour the mixture into the tin and spread evenly. Leave until just set, then mark into squares. Leave to set completely before cutting into squares and removing from the tin. Store in an airtight container in a cool place.

Nutritional information: Energy 112kcal/472kJ; Protein 1.5g; Carbohydrate 18.2g, of which sugars 18.1g; Fat 4.2g, of which saturates 2.1g; Cholesterol 7mg; Calcium 39mg; Fibre 0.2g; Sodium 35mg.

Chocolate-coated nut brittle

Take equal amounts of pecan nuts and almonds, set them in crisp caramel, then add a dark chocolate coating for a sweet that's sensational.

MAKES 20–24 PIECES

115g/4oz/1 cup mixed pecan halves and whole almonds
115g/4oz/¹/₂ cup caster (superfine) sugar
60ml/4 tbsp water
200g/7oz dark (bittersweet) chocolate, broken into squares

1 Lightly grease a baking sheet with butter or oil. Mix the nuts, sugar and water in a heavy pan. Place the pan over a gentle heat, stirring without boiling until the sugar has dissolved.

2 Bring to the boil, then lower the heat to medium and cook until the mixture turns a rich golden brown and registers 148°C/300°F on a sugar thermometer. To test without a thermometer, drop a few drops of the mixture into a cup of iced water. The mixture should become brittle enough to snap with your fingers.

3 Quickly remove the pan from the heat and turn the mixture on to the prepared baking sheet, spreading it evenly. Leave until completely cold and hard.

4 Break the nut brittle into bitesize pieces. Melt the chocolate in a heatproof bowl over simmering water and dip the pieces to half-coat them. Leave on a sheet of baking parchment to set.

Nutritional information: Energy 94kcal/395kJ; Protein 0.9g; Carbohydrate 10.6g, of which sugars 10.4g; Fat 5.7g, of which saturates 1.7g; Cholesterol 1mg; Calcium 8mg; Fibre 0.4g; Sodium 1mg.

Easy chocolate hazelnut fudge

You can ring the changes with this scrumptious fudge by making a second batch using white chocolate. Pour this on top of the first (after it's set) to make two-tone fudge.

MAKES 16 SQUARES

150ml/¼ pint/²/₃ cup evaporated milk
350g/12oz/1½ cups sugar
large pinch of salt
50g/2oz/½ cup hazelnuts, halved
350g/12oz/2 cups plain (semisweet)
    chocolate chips

1 Generously grease a 20cm/8in square cake tin (pan).

2 Place the evaporated milk, sugar and salt in a heavy pan. Bring to the boil over a medium heat, stirring constantly. Lower the heat and simmer gently, stirring, for 5 minutes.

3 Remove from the heat and add the hazelnuts and chocolate chips. Stir until the chocolate has melted.

4 Quickly pour the fudge mixture into the prepared tin and spread evenly. Leave to cool and set.

5 When the chocolate hazelnut fudge has set, use a sharp knife to cut it into 2.5cm/1in squares.

6 Store the fudge squares in a large airtight container in a cool place, separating the layers of fudge with baking parchment.

Nutritional information: Energy 231kcal/975kJ; Protein 2.4g; Carbohydrate 38.3g, of which sugars 38g; Fat 8.7g, of which saturates 4.2g; Cholesterol 3mg; Calcium 48mg; Fibre 0.8g; Sodium 14mg.

Chocolate nut clusters

These bitesize clusters contain a mix of hazelnuts, pecans, walnuts, brazil nuts and peanuts enveloped in smooth dark chocolate. Simply delicious.

MAKES ABOUT 30

525ml/21fl oz/2¹⁄₂ cups double (heavy) cream
25g/1oz/2 tbsp unsalted (sweet) butter, cut into small pieces
350ml/12fl oz/1¹⁄₂ cups golden (light corn) syrup
200g/7oz/scant 1 cup sugar
75g/3oz/¹⁄₂ cup soft light brown sugar
pinch of salt
15ml/1 tbsp vanilla extract
350g/12oz/3 cups mixed hazelnuts, pecans, walnuts, brazil nuts and unsalted peanuts
400g/14oz plain (semisweet) chocolate, chopped into small pieces
15g/¹⁄₂oz/1 tbsp white vegetable fat (shortening)

1 Oil two baking sheets. In a pan, gently heat the cream, butter, golden syrup, sugars and salt, stirring occasionally, until the sugars dissolve and the butter melts.

2 Bring to the boil and continue cooking, stirring frequently, for 1 hour, until the caramel reaches 119°C/238°F on a sugar thermometer, or until a piece of caramel dropped into a cup of iced water forms a hard ball.

3 Plunge the bottom of the pan into cold water to stop cooking. Cool slightly, and stir in the vanilla, then the nuts, until well coated.

4 With an oiled tablespoon, drop spoonfuls of nut mixture on to the prepared sheets, about 2.5cm/1in apart. If the mixture hardens, return to the heat to soften. Chill for 30 minutes, until hardened.

5 Transfer to a wire rack placed over a baking sheet. In a pan over a low heat, melt the chocolate with the white vegetable fat, stirring until smooth. Set aside to cool slightly.

6 Spoon chocolate over each cluster, to cover them completely. Allow to set for 2 hours, or until hard. Store in an airtight container.

Nutritional information: Energy 311kcal/1298kJ; Protein 2.7g; Carbohydrate 28.3g, of which sugars 27.9g; Fat 21.6g, of which saturates 9.2g; Cholesterol 27mg; Calcium 36mg; Fibre 1.1g; Sodium 46mg.

Mexican hot chocolate

In Mexico, this drink is traditionally whisked with a carved wooden beater called a molinillo, but a modern blender works just as well.

SERVES 4

1 litre/1³⁄4 pints/4 cups milk
1 cinnamon stick
2 whole cloves
115g/4oz dark (bittersweet) chocolate, broken
    into squares
2–3 drops almond extract

1 Heat the milk gently with the spices in a pan until almost boiling, then stir in the chocolate over a medium heat until melted.

2 Strain into a blender, add the almond extract and whizz on high speed for about 30 seconds until frothy. Alternatively, whisk the mixture with a hand-held electric mixer or wire whisk.

3 Pour into heatproof glasses and serve immediately.

COOK'S TIP
If you don't have whole cinnamon and cloves, add a pinch of each of the ground spices to the mixture before whisking.

Nutritional information: Energy 220kcal/924kJ; Protein 8.1g; Carbohydrate 25.3g, of which sugars 25.1g; Fat 10.4g, of which saturates 6.4g; Cholesterol 13mg; Calcium 248mg; Fibre 0.6g; Sodium 88mg.

Mint chocolate sticks

Turn the lights down low, curl up on the couch and pamper yourself with these delicious bitesize chocolate sticks.

MAKES ABOUT 80

115g/4oz/¹⁄2 cup sugar
150ml/¹⁄4 pint/²⁄3 cup water
2.5ml/¹⁄2 tsp peppermint extract
200g/7oz dark (bittersweet) chocolate, broken into squares
60ml/4 tbsp toasted desiccated (dry unsweetened
    shredded) coconut

1 Lightly oil a large baking sheet. Place the sugar and water in a pan and heat gently, stirring occasionally, until the sugar has dissolved.

2 Bring to the boil and boil rapidly without stirring until the syrup registers 137°C/280°F on a sugar thermometer. Remove from the heat and add the peppermint extract, then pour on to the oiled baking sheet and leave until set and completely cold.

3 Break up the peppermint mixture into a bowl and use the end of a rolling pin to crush it into small pieces.

4 Melt the chocolate in a heatproof bowl set over a pan of simmering water. Remove from the heat and stir in the mint pieces and coconut.

5 Lay a 30 x 25cm/12 x 10in sheet of baking parchment on a surface. Spread the chocolate mixture over the paper, leaving a narrow border all around, to make a rectangle measuring 25 x 20cm/10 x 8in. Leave to set. When firm, cut into thin sticks with a sharp knife.

Nutritional information: Energy 23kcal/96kJ; Protein 0.2g; Carbohydrate 3.1g, of which sugars 3.1g; Fat 1.2g, of which saturates 0.8g; Cholesterol 0mg; Calcium 2mg; Fibre 0.2g; Sodium 0mg.

Irish chocolate velvet

Smooth and silky, this truly delectable drink is infused with Irish whiskey and topped with whipped cream.

SERVES 4

120ml/4fl oz/$^{1}/_{2}$ cup double (heavy) cream
400ml/14fl oz/1$^{3}/_{4}$ cups milk
115g/4oz milk chocolate, broken into squares
30ml/2 tbsp unsweetened cocoa powder
60ml/4 tbsp Irish whiskey
whipped cream, for topping
chocolate curls, to decorate

1 Whip the cream in a bowl until it is thick enough to hold its shape.

2 Place the milk and chocolate in a pan and heat gently, stirring, until the chocolate has melted.

3 Whisk in the cocoa, then bring to the boil, remove from the heat and add the cream and Irish whiskey.

4 Pour quickly into four heatproof mugs or glasses and top each serving with a generous spoonful of whipped cream. Decorate with chocolate curls and serve.

Nutritional information: Energy 390kcal/1623kJ; Protein 7.5g; Carbohydrate 22.4g, of which sugars 21.6g; Fat 28.3g, of which saturates 17.3g; Cholesterol 54mg; Calcium 208mg; Fibre 1.1g; Sodium 145mg.

Mint chocolate cooler

Many chocolate drinks are warm and comforting, but this one is really refreshing – ideal for a hot summer's day.

SERVES 4

60ml/4 tbsp drinking chocolate powder
400ml/14fl oz/1$^{3}/_{4}$ cups chilled milk
150ml/5fl oz/$^{2}/_{3}$ cup natural (plain) yogurt
2.5ml/$^{1}/_{2}$ tsp peppermint extract
4 scoops chocolate ice cream
mint leaves and chocolate shapes,
    to decorate

1 Place the drinking chocolate in a small pan and stir in about 120ml/4fl oz/$^{1}/_{2}$ cup of the milk. Heat gently, stirring, until almost boiling, then remove from the heat.

2 Pour into a cold bowl or large jug (pitcher) and whisk in the remaining milk, yogurt and peppermint extract. Leave to cool, then chill.

3 Pour the mixture into four tall glasses and top each with a scoop of ice cream. Decorate with mint leaves and chocolate shapes. Serve immediately.

Nutritional information: Energy 231kcal/968kJ; Protein 8.1g; Carbohydrate 27.9g, of which sugars 27.5g; Fat 10.5g, of which saturates 6.3g; Cholesterol 6mg; Calcium 247mg; Fibre 0g; Sodium 138mg.

Chocolate toppings and decorations

Whether you are looking for a delicious buttercream icing to frost your cake or an indulgent chocolate sauce to pour over vanilla ice cream, you will find it in the following pages. There are also decoration ideas for chocolate curls, scrolls, squiggles and leaves to add that extra-special finishing touch to any dessert.

Simple buttercream

A sweet and creamy icing that is highly versatile and easy to make.

ENOUGH TO FILL A 20CM/8IN ROUND CAKE

75g/3oz unsalted (sweet) butter or soft margarine
225g/8oz/1½ cups icing (confectioners') sugar
5ml/1 tsp vanilla extract
10–15ml/2–3 tsp milk

1 If using butter, allow it to come to room temperature so that it can easily be creamed. Sift the icing sugar. Put the butter or margarine in a bowl. Add about a quarter of the icing sugar and beat with a hand-held electric mixer until fluffy.

2 Using a metal spoon, add the remaining sifted icing sugar, a little at a time, beating well with the electric mixer after each addition. Icing sugar is so fine that if you add too much of it at one time, it tends to fly out of the bowl.

3 Beat in 5ml/1 tsp of the milk. The mixture should be light and creamy, with a spreadable consistency. Add the vanilla extract, then more milk if necessary, but not too much, or the resulting mixture will be too sloppy. Use as a filling or topping on layer cakes and cupcakes.

Nutritional information: Energy 992kcal/4225kJ; Protein 15.5g; Carbohydrate 236.7g, of which sugars 236.2g; Fat 4.7g, of which saturates 0.7g; Cholesterol 41mg; Calcium 141mg; Fibre 0.2g; Sodium 54mg.

Chocolate buttercream

A tasty alternative to simple buttercream. Use it for filling and frosting.

ENOUGH TO FILL A 20CM/8IN ROUND CAKE

75g/3oz/6 tbsp unsalted (sweet) butter or margarine, softened
175g/6oz/1½ cups icing (confectioners') sugar
15ml/1 tbsp unsweetened cocoa powder
2.5ml/½ tsp vanilla extract

Place all the ingredients in a large bowl and beat well to a smooth, spreadable consistency.

VARIATIONS

Coffee buttercream: Stir 10ml/2 tsp instant coffee into 15ml/ 1 tbsp boiling water. Beat into the icing instead of the milk.

Mocha buttercream: Stir 5ml/1 tsp cocoa powder into 10ml/2 tsp boiling water. Beat into the icing. Add a little coffee extract.

Orange buttercream: Use orange juice instead of the milk and vanilla extract, and add 10ml/2tsp finely grated orange rind. Omit the rind if using the icing for piping.

Nutritional information: Energy 1291kcal/5416kJ; Protein 3.8g; Carbohydrate 185.3g, of which sugars 183.6g; Fat 64.5g, of which saturates 1.9g; Cholesterol 0mg; Calcium 115mg; Fibre 1.8g; Sodium 753mg.

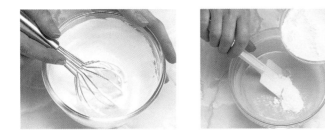  

White chocolate frosting

A fluffy, rich, white frosting perfect for cakes and gateaux.

ENOUGH TO COVER A 20CM/8IN ROUND CAKE

175g/6oz white chocolate, broken into squares
75g/3oz/6 tbsp unsalted (sweet) butter
115g/4oz/1 cup icing (confectioners') sugar
90ml/6 tbsp double (heavy) cream

1 Melt the chocolate with the butter in a heatproof bowl over simmering water. Remove from the heat and beat in the icing sugar.

2 Whip the cream in a separate bowl until it just holds its shape, then beat into the chocolate mixture. Allow the mixture to cool, stirring occasionally, until it begins to hold its shape. Use immediately.

VARIATION
For a special occasion cake, stir in a tablespoon of brandy or your favourite liqueur.

Nutritional information: Energy 2383kcal/9935kJ; Protein 16.5g; Carbohydrate 224.2g, of which sugars 224.2g; Fat 164.1g, of which saturates 101.3g; Cholesterol 283mg; Calcium 591mg; Fibre 0g; Sodium 674mg.

Chocolate ganache

A luxurious and creamy frosting for covering gateaux and desserts.

ENOUGH TO COVER A 23CM/9IN ROUND CAKE

250ml/8fl oz/1 cup double (heavy) cream
225g/8oz plain (semisweet) chocolate, broken into squares

1 Heat the cream and chocolate together in a pan over a low heat, stirring frequently until the chocolate has melted.

2 Pour into a bowl, leave to cool, then whisk until the mixture begins to hold its shape.

Nutritional information: Energy 2388kcal/9911kJ; Protein 15.3g; Carbohydrate 147.1g, of which sugars 145.1g; Fat 197.3g, of which saturates 121.3g; Cholesterol 356mg; Calcium 197mg; Fibre 5.6g; Sodium 69mg.

Glossy chocolate sauce

Delicious poured over ice cream or on hot or cold desserts.

SERVES 6

115g/4oz/¹/₂ cup caster (superfine) sugar
60ml/4 tbsp water
175g/6oz plain (semisweet) chocolate, broken into squares
30ml/2 tbsp unsalted (sweet) butter
30ml/2 tbsp brandy or orange juice

1 Place the sugar and water in a pan and heat gently, stirring occasionally, until the sugar has dissolved.

2 Stir in the chocolate, a few squares at a time, until melted, then add the butter in the same way. Do not allow the sauce to boil. Stir in the brandy or orange juice and serve warm.

COOK'S TIP
This sauce freezes well. Pour it into a freezer-proof container, seal, label and freeze for up to 3 months. Thaw at room temperature.

Nutritional information: Energy 273kcal/1144kJ; Protein 1.6g; Carbohydrate 38.6g, of which sugars 38.3g; Fat 12.3g, of which saturates 7.5g; Cholesterol 12mg; Calcium 21mg; Fibre 0.7g; Sodium 33mg.

White chocolate sauce

Rich and sweet, this makes a lovely contrast to a dark, bitter chocolate mousse or pudding.

SERVES 6

150ml/¹/₄ pint/²/₃ cup double (heavy) cream
150g/5oz white chocolate, broken into squares
30ml/2 tbsp brandy or Cointreau

1 Heat the cream in a pan over a low heat until almost boiling.

2 Stir in the chocolate, a few squares at a time, until melted and smooth. Remove from the heat and stir in the brandy or Cointreau just before serving.

VARIATIONS
White mocha sauce: stir in 30ml/2 tbsp strong black coffee just before serving.

Coconut chocolate cream sauce: stir in 45ml/3 tbsp powdered or liquid coconut cream just before serving.

Nutritional information: Energy 267kcal/1109kJ; Protein 2.4g; Carbohydrate 15g, of which sugars 15g; Fat 21.2g, of which saturates 13g; Cholesterol 34mg; Calcium 80mg; Fibre 0g; Sodium 33mg.

Chocolate fondant

This versatile icing is great for covering cakes and for cutting out decorative shapes.

MAKES ENOUGH TO COVER AND DECORATE A 9-INCH ROUND CAKE

350g/12oz dark (bittersweet) chocolate, chopped into
    small pieces
125ml/1/2 cup liquid glucose
2 egg whites
800g/30oz/7 cups icing (confectioners') sugar

1 Put the chocolate and glucose in a heatproof bowl. Place over a pan of barely simmering water and melt, stirring occasionally until smooth. Remove the bowl from the heat and cool slightly.

2 In a grease-free bowl, whisk the egg whites with a hand-held electric mixer until soft peaks form, then stir into the chocolate mixture with 3 tablespoons of the icing sugar.

3 Continue to beat the fondant, gradually adding enough of the remaining icing sugar to make a stiff paste. Wrap in cling film (plastic wrap) if not using immediately.

Nutritional information: Energy 1664kcal/6950kJ; Protein 22.8g; Carbohydrate 171.5g, of which sugars 34.7g; Fat 103.3g, of which saturates 64.1g; Cholesterol 245mg; Calcium 321mg; Fibre 9.1g; Sodium 989mg.

Chocolate shortcrust pastry

A rich, dark, chocolate-flavoured pastry for sweet flans and tarts.

MAKES ENOUGH TO LINE A 9-INCH TART TIN (PAN)

115g/4oz plain (semisweet) chocolate, broken into squares
225g/8oz/2 cups plain (all-purpose) flour
115g/4oz/1/2 cup unsalted (sweet) butter
15–30ml/1–2 tbsp cold water

1 Melt the chocolate in a heatproof bowl over simmering water. Allow to cool but not set.

2 Place the flour in a mixing bowl. Rub in the butter until the mixture resembles fine breadcrumbs.

3 Make a well in the centre of the mixture. Add the cooled chocolate, with just enough cold water to mix to a firm dough.

Nutritional information: Energy 2209kcal/9238kJ; Protein 27.6g; Carbohydrate 248.5g, of which sugars 76.1g; Fat 129.7g, of which saturates 79.7g; Cholesterol 252mg; Calcium 374mg; Fibre 9.8g; Sodium 711mg.

Melting chocolate

If chocolate is being melted on its own, all the equipment must be completely dry, as water may cause the chocolate to thicken and become a stiff paste. For this reason, do not cover chocolate during or after melting it, as condensation could form. If chocolate does thicken, add a little pure white vegetable fat (not butter or margarine) and mix well. If this does not work, start again. Do not discard the thickened chocolate; melt it with cream to make a sauce.

With or without liquid, chocolate should be melted very slowly. It is easily burned or scorched, and then develops a bad flavour. If any steam gets into the chocolate, it can turn into a solid mass. If this happens, stir in a little pure white vegetable fat. Dark chocolate should not be heated above 50°C/120°F. Milk and white chocolate should not be heated above 45°C/110°F. Take particular care when melting white chocolate, which clogs very easily when subjected to heat.

Never allow water or steam to come into contact with melting chocolate; it may cause it to stiffen. Remember to use high-quality chocolate for the best results. Look for the cocoa solids content on the back of the wrapper: the higher the better.

Melting chocolate over simmering water

1 Chop the chocolate into small pieces with a sharp knife to enable it to melt quickly and evenly.

2 Put the chopped chocolate in the top of a double boiler or in a heatproof bowl set over a pan of barely simmering water. Make sure that the bowl does not touch the water.

3 Heat gently until the chocolate is completely melted and smooth, stirring occasionally. Remove the pan from the heat and stir.

Melting chocolate over direct heat or in the oven

When a recipe recommends melting chocolate with a liquid such as milk, cream or even butter, this can be done over direct heat in a pan.

1 Chop the chocolate into small pieces. Choose a heavy pan. Add the chocolate and liquid and melt over a low heat, stirring frequently, until the chocolate is melted and the mixture is smooth. Remove the pan from the heat immediately. This method is also used for making sauces, icings and some sweets.

2 Chocolate can also be melted in a very low oven. Preheat the oven to 110°C/225°F/Gas ¼. Put the chocolate in an ovenproof bowl and place in the oven for a few minutes.

3 Remove the chocolate before it is completely melted and stir until it is smooth.

Melting chocolate in the microwave

When using this method, be sure to check the chocolate at frequent intervals during the cooking time. These times are for a 650–700W oven and are approximate, as microwave ovens vary.

1 Place 115g/4oz chopped or broken plain (semisweet) or dark (bittersweet) chocolate in a microwave-safe bowl and microwave on medium for about 2 minutes. The same quantity of milk or white chocolate should be melted on low for about 2 minutes.

2 Check the chocolate frequently during the cooking time. The chocolate will not change shape, but it will start to look shiny. It must then be removed from the microwave and stirred continuously with a wooden spoon until it is completely melted and smooth.

Tempering chocolate

Tempering is the process of gently heating and cooling chocolate to stabilize the emulsification of cocoa solids and butterfat. This technique is used by professionals handling couverture chocolate. It allows the chocolate to be kept at room temperature for several weeks without losing its crispness and shiny surface. All solid chocolate is tempered in production, but once melted loses its "temper" and must be tempered again unless it is to be used immediately.

1 Break up the chocolate into small pieces and place it in the top of a double boiler or a heatproof bowl over a pan of simmering water. Heat gently until just melted.

2 Remove the chocolate from the heat. Spoon about three-quarters of the melted chocolate on to a marble slab or other cool, smooth, non-porous work surface.

3 With a flexible plastic scraper or palette knife, spread the chocolate thinly, then scoop it up before spreading it again.

4 Repeat the sequence, keeping the chocolate constantly on the move, for about 5 minutes.

5 Using a chocolate thermometer, keep checking the temperature of the chocolate as you work it. As soon as the temperature registers 28°C/82°F, put the chocolate back into the bowl and stir into the remaining chocolate.

6 With the addition of the hot chocolate, the temperature should now be 32°C/90°F, making the chocolate ready for use.

7 To test whether it is ready, drop a little of the chocolate from a spoon on to the marble; it should set quickly.

Piping with chocolate

Pipe chocolate directly on to a cake, or on to baking parchment to make run-outs, small outlined shapes or irregular designs. After melting the chocolate, allow to cool slightly so it just coats the back of a spoon. When it is the right consistency, you need to work fast, as the chocolate will set quickly. Use a paper piping bag and keep the pressure very tight, as the chocolate will flow readily without encouragement.

Making a paper piping bag

A non-stick paper cone is ideal for piping small amounts of messy liquids like chocolate, as it is small, easy to handle and disposable, unlike a conventional piping bag, which will need cleaning.

1 Fold a square of baking parchment in half to form a triangle. With the triangle point facing you, fold the left corner down to the centre.

2 Fold the right corner down and wrap it around the folded left corner to form a cone. Fold the ends into the cone.

3 Spoon the chocolate into the cone and fold the top edges over. Snip off the end of the point neatly to make a hole, about 3mm/⅛in in diameter.

4 Another method is to use a small plastic bag. Place a piping nozzle in one corner of the bag, so that it is in the correct position for piping. Fill as above, squeeze the filling into one corner and twist the top to seal. Snip off the corner of the bag, so the tip of the nozzle emerges, and squeeze gently to pipe.

Chocolate drizzles

You can have great fun making random shapes out of chocolate or, with a steady hand, special designs that will look great on cakes or biscuits.

1 Melt the chocolate and pour it into a paper cone or small piping bag fitted with a very small plain nozzle. Drizzle the chocolate on to a baking sheet lined with baking parchment to make small, self-contained lattice shapes, such as circles or squares. Allow the chocolate to set for 30 minutes then peel off the paper.

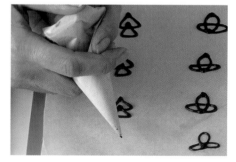

2 Chocolate can be used in many designs, such as flowers or butterflies. Use baking parchment as tracing paper and pipe the chocolate over the chosen design or decorative shape.

3 To make butterfly shapes, pipe chocolate on to individually cut squares of baking parchment and wait until it just begins to set. Place the butterfly shape between the cups of an egg carton, or across a folded piece of cardboard, so it is bent in the centre, creating the butterfly shape. Chill until needed.

Piping on to cakes

This method looks very effective on top of a cake iced with coffee glacé icing.

1 Melt 50g/2oz each of white and plain (semisweet) chocolate in separate bowls, and allow to cool slightly.

2 Place the chocolates in separate paper piping bags. Using scissors, cut a small piece off the pointed end of each bag in a straight line.

3 Hold each piping bag in turn above the surface of the cake and pipe the chocolates all over as shown. Alternatively, pipe a freehand design in one continuous curvy line, first with one bag of chocolate, then the other.

Storing chocolate

Chocolate can be stored successfully for up to a year if the conditions are favourable. This means a dry place with a temperature of around 68°F. At higher temperatures the chocolate may develop white streaks as the fat comes to the surface. When storing chocolate, keep it cool and dry. Place it inside an airtight container, away from strong smelling foods. Check the "best before" date on the pack.

Piping curls

Make lots of these curly shapes and store them in a cool place ready for using as cake decorations.

1 Melt 115g/4oz chocolate and allow to cool slightly. Cover a rolling pin with baking parchment, and attach it with tape. Fill a paper piping bag with the chocolate and cut a small piece off the pointed end in a straight line.

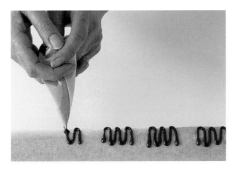

2 Pipe lines of chocolate back and forth over the baking parchment.

3 Leave the piped curls to set in a cool place, then carefully peel off the baking parchment.

Feathering or marbling chocolate

These techniques are the easiest and most effective ways of decorating the top of a cake.

1 Melt two contrasting colours of chocolate and spread one over the cake or surface to be decorated.

2 Spoon the contrasting chocolate into a piping bag and pipe lines or swirls over the chocolate base.

3 Working quickly before the chocolate sets, draw a skewer or cocktail stick through the swirls to create a feathered or marbled effect.

Chocolate decorations

These decorations are useful for all kinds of cakes and desserts. If you are making chunky curls, scrolls or cut-outs, you can also use dark and white chocolate marbled together.

Grated chocolate

Chocolate can be grated by hand or in a food processor. Make sure you grate it at the correct temperature.

1 Chill the chocolate and hold it with a piece of folded foil or paper towel to prevent it melting. Hold a hand- or box-grater over a large plate and grate with an even pressure.

2 A food processor with a metal blade can also be used to grate chocolate, but be sure the chocolate is soft enough to be pierced with a sharp knife. Cut the chocolate into small pieces and, with the machine running, drop the pieces through the feeder tube until fine shavings are produced. Use the grater attachment and pusher to feed the chocolate through the processor, for larger shavings.

Mini chocolate curls

Simple chocolate curls can make an ideal decoration for many different desserts and cakes, and they can be made from any type of chocolate.

These curls can be made very quickly using a vegetable peeler, and can be stored for several weeks in an airtight container in a cool, dry place.

1 Bring a thick piece or bar of chocolate to room temperature. (Chocolate that is too cold will "grate", or, if too warm, will slice.) With a swivel-bladed peeler held over a plate or baking sheet, pull the blade firmly along the edge of the chocolate and allow curls to fall on to the plate or baking sheet in a single layer.

2 Use a skewer or cocktail stick (toothpick) to carefully transfer the curls to the dessert or cake.

Chunky chocolate curls

These curls are best made with dark chocolate that has been melted with pure white vegetable fat (about 5ml/1 tsp per 25g/1oz of chocolate), which keeps the chocolate from hardening completely.

1 Melt 175g/6oz plain (semisweet) chocolate with 30ml/2 tbsp pure white vegetable fat, stirring continuously until smooth.

2 Pour into a small rectangular or square tin (pan) lined with foil or baking parchment to produce a block about 2.5cm/1in thick. Chill until set.

3 Allow the block to come to room temperature, remove it from the tin, then hold it with a piece of folded foil or paper towel (to stop it melting) and use a swivel-bladed peeler to produce short chunky curls. The block of chocolate can also be grated.

Chocolate scrolls or short round curls

Temper dark or white chocolate, or use chocolate prepared for Chunky Chocolate Curls to produce these decorative scrolls.

1 Pour the prepared chocolate evenly on to a marble slab or the back of a baking sheet. Using a palette knife, or metal spatula, spread to about 3mm/⅛in thick and allow to set for about 30 minutes until just firm.

2 To make long scrolls, use the blade of a long, sharp knife on the surface of the chocolate, and, with both hands, push away from your body at a 25°–45° angle to scrape off a thin layer of chocolate. Twist the handle of the knife about a quarter of a circle to make a slightly wider scroll. Use a teaspoon to make cup-shaped curls. A variety of shapes and sizes can be produced, depending on the temperature of the chocolate and the tool used.

Chocolate cut-outs

You can make abstract shapes, or circles, squares and diamonds, by cutting them out freehand with a sharp knife. If you do not feel confident about cutting chocolate cut-outs freehand, use biscuit or aspic cutters. Cut-outs look good around the sides of cakes or gateaux. Space them at regular intervals or allow them to overlap.

1 Cover a baking sheet with baking parchment and tape down at each corner. Melt 115g/4oz dark, milk or white chocolate. Pour the chocolate on to the baking parchment.

2 Spread the chocolate over the baking parchment in an even layer with a palette knife. Allow it to stand until the surface of the chocolate is firm enough to cut, but not so hard that it will break. It should no longer feel sticky when touched lightly with your finger.

3 Press the cutter firmly through the chocolate and lift off the paper with a palette knife. Try not to touch the surface of the chocolate or you will leave marks on it and spoil its appearance.

4 The finished shapes can be left plain or piped with a contrasting chocolate for a decorative effect.

5 Abstract shapes can be cut with a knife, freehand. These types of shapes look particularly effective pressed on to the sides of a cake which has been iced with plain or chocolate buttercream.

Chocolate squiggles

Melt a quantity of chocolate and, using a metal spatula, spread it fairly thinly and evenly over a cool, smooth surface. Leave until just set. Draw a citrus zester firmly across the surface to remove curls or "squiggles" of the chocolate.

Chocolate-dipped fruit

Strawberries, grapes, cherries and other small fruits taste absolutely delicious when fully or partially coated in chocolate, as do fresh mandarin segments.

Fruit for dipping should be ripe but not soft, and clean and dry. Whole nuts such as almonds or brazils can also be dipped. They can be served on their own as a tasty snack, or can be used as very effective decorations on top of cakes or desserts.

SERVES 6

115g/4oz/¹/₂ cup caster (superfine) sugar
60ml/4 tbsp water
175g/6oz plain (semisweet) chocolate, broken into squares
30ml/2 tbsp unsalted (sweet) butter
30ml/2 tbsp brandy or orange juice

1 Melt the chocolate over simmering water and remove from the heat.

2 Dip the fruits or nuts fully or halfway into the chocolate and allow the excess to drip off.

3 Place on a baking sheet lined with baking parchment and leave until completely set.

Chocolate leaves

You can use any fresh, non-toxic leaf with distinct veins, to make these decorations. If small leaves are required, for decorating petits fours, for example, use mint or lemon balm leaves.

1 Wash the leaves thoroughly then allow to dry on kitchen paper.

2 Melt plain (semisweet) or white chocolate over simmering water.

3 Use a pastry brush or spoon to carefully coat the veined side of each leaf completely with chocolate.

4 Place the coated leaves chocolate-side up on a baking sheet lined with baking parchment to set.

5 Starting at the stem end, gently peel away each leaf in turn. Store the chocolate leaves in a cool place.

BELOW: *Chocolate leaves make an unusual topping for a cake or dessert.*

Chocolate baskets

These impressive baskets make very pretty, edible containers for mousse, ice cream or tiramisù.

MAKES 6

175g/6oz plain (semisweet), milk or
white chocolate
25g/1oz/2 tbsp butter

1 Cut out six 15cm/6in rounds from baking parchment.

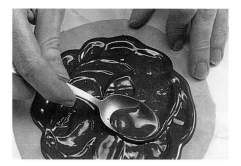

2 Melt the chocolate with the butter in a heatproof bowl over simmering water. Stir until smooth. Spoon one-sixth of the chocolate over each round, using a teaspoon to spread it to within 2cm/³⁄₄in of the edge.

3 Carefully lift each covered parchment round and drape it over an upturned cup or ramekin, curving the edges of the parchment to create a frilled effect.

4 Leave until completely set, then carefully lift off the chocolate shape and peel away the paper.

5 For a different effect, try brushing the chocolate over the parchment, leaving the edges jagged. Invert the chocolate baskets on individual dessert plates and gently peel off the paper. Add your chosen filling, taking great care not to break the chocolate.

BELOW: *Chocolate baskets can be used to hold desserts, such as ice cream.*

Chocolate cups

Large or small cupcake papers or sweet (candy) cases can be used to make delicate chocolate cups, which can then be filled with ice cream, mousse or truffles. Use double paper cases inside each other to give extra support.

1 Melt the chocolate. Using a paintbrush or pastry brush, carefully coat the cases, making sure that you completely cover the bottom and sides of the paper cases.

2 Allow the first layer of chocolate to set, and then repeat the process once or twice more to build up a few layers. Allow to set for several hours or preferably overnight.

3 When they are completely set, carefully peel off the double layer of paper cases, then place the chocolate cups on a baking sheet and fill as desired.

The guide to chocolate

This section looks at the history of chocolate, how it is manufactured into the food we know and love and the different types available. There is also a fascinating study of the effects of chocolate on our bodies and minds, and people's attempts to understand why it arouses such strong desires.

The history of chocolate

The origins of the solid, sensuous and, to some, addictive substance we know as chocolate are rooted in New World prehistory, in the mysterious realm of the Olmec and the Maya. It was these ancient Mesoamerican civilizations living in the heart of equatorial Central America that were responsible for cultivating the tree from which chocolate is derived.

THE OLMEC

Approximately three thousand years ago, the Olmec people, one of the earliest Mesoamerican civilizations, occupied an area of tropical forests south of Veracruz on the Gulf of Mexico. Modern linguists have managed to reconstruct the ancient Olmec vocabulary and have found that it includes the word "cacao". Given the cacao tree's requirement for hot, humid and shady conditions, such as the land of the Olmecs, many historians are certain that the first civilization to cultivate the tree was that of the Olmecs, and not the Aztecs, as is commonly believed.

THE MAYA

Around the 4th century AD, several centuries after the demise of the Olmec, the Maya had established themselves in a large region just south of present-day Mexico. The humid climate there was perfect for the cacao tree, and it flourished in the shade of the tropical forest. The Maya called the tree *cacahuaquchtl* "tree": as far as they were concerned, there was no other tree worth naming. They believed that the tree belonged to the gods and that the pods growing from its trunk were an offering from the gods to humankind.

The period around AD300, known as the Classic Mayan civilization, was a time of great artistic, intellectual and spiritual development. The Maya built magnificent stone palaces and temples, carving into the sacred walls images of cacao pods – for them the symbol of life and fertility.

The Maya were the originators of a bitter brew made from cacao beans. This was a luxury drink enjoyed by kings and noblemen, and also used to solemnize sacred rituals. In their books, the Maya describe several ways of making and flavouring the brew. An early picture shows the dark brown liquid being poured from one vessel to another to produce an all-important froth. Various spices were used as flavourings, the favourite being chilli.

LEFT: *The Maya wrote their books on folding screens of bark paper. These two pages show a black-faced merchant god with cacao growers.*

RIGHT: *A mosaic of Quetzalcoatl, who, according to legend, brought the cacao bean as a gift to humankind.*

More evidence of Maya use of cacao survives on the many painted vessels that have been unearthed from their burial grounds. A tomb excavated in Guatemala in 1984 contained several vessels obviously used for chocolate drinking. One exotic and beautiful specimen bears the Mayan symbol for chocolate on its lid and was found still to contain residues of the drink.

THE TOLTECS AND AZTECS

After the mysterious fall of the Mayan empire in around AD900, the gifted and supremely civilized Toltecs, later followed by the Aztecs, settled in former Mayan territory. Quetzalcoatl, the Toltec king, was also believed to be the god of air, whose mission was to bring the seeds of the cacao tree from Eden to humankind and teach mortals how to cultivate crops.

Due to political uprisings, Quetzalcoatl and his followers left the capital and fled south to the Yucatán. During a period of ill health he was persuaded to drink a mysterious cure, which, in fact, drove him insane. Convinced he

must leave his kingdom, Quetzalcoatl sailed away on a raft, promising to return in a preordained year to reclaim his kingdom. The legend became part of Aztec mythology, and astrologers predicted that in 1519 a white-faced king would return to release his people. This belief was to influence the whole future of the New World.

THE SPANISH ADVENTURERS

Although the Spanish explorer Hernán Cortés is generally considered to be the first European to recognize the potential of Aztec chocolate, the initial discovery must be attributed to Christopher Columbus. In 1502, Columbus reached the island of Guanaja off the Honduran coast. The story goes that he was greeted by Aztecs, who offered him a sackful of what looked like large almonds in exchange for some of his own merchandise. The Aztecs explained that a drink, tchocolatl (or xocolatl), could be made with these beans. Columbus and his crew found the resulting concoction rather repellent but nevertheless took some beans back to Spain for curiosity value, little realizing their future worth.

CACAO AS CURRENCY

When Hernán Cortés arrived in the New World seventeen years later, Montezuma II, the then Aztec Emperor, believed Cortés to be a reincarnation of Quetzalcoatl, the exiled Toltec god-king whose return had been predicted to take place in the same year. The confusion made it easy for Cortés to gain access to Tenochtitlán, the Aztec capital, where Montezuma received him and his men with a royal welcome. The emperor offered them numerous gifts, including a cacao plantation, and an extravagant banquet was prepared in their honour.

Montezuma eventually realized that he had made a mistake and had wrongly identified the Spaniard. Immediately recognizing the insecurity of his position, Cortés enlisted the help of sympathetic natives and managed to take Montezuma prisoner. Within the space of two or three years, he

Theobroma cacao

The eighteenth-century Swedish botanist Linnaeus, who invented the binomial system of classification for all living things, later named the tree *Theobroma cacao*, meaning "drink of the gods", from the Greek *theos* (god) and *broma* (beverage). He felt it deserved a name that reflected the Mayan belief that the tree belonged to the gods, rather than the New World name of cacao or chocolate tree.

brought about the downfall of the Aztec kingdom. Unlike Columbus, Cortés quickly realized the enormous economic value of the cacao bean, both as food and as a form of currency. A contemporary of Cortés reported that a slave could be bought for one hundred cacao beans, the services of a prostitute for ten, and a rabbit for four. The Jesuit, Pedro Martyre de Angleria, called the beans "pecuniary almonds" and described them as "blessed money, which exempts its possessors from avarice, since it cannot be hoarded or hidden underground". It is presumed that he was referring to the fact that the beans could not be stored for long without rotting.

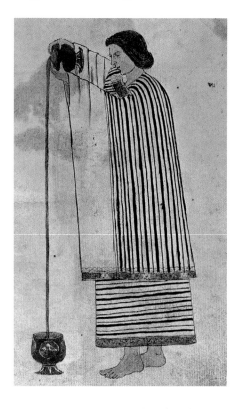

ABOVE: *Aztecs poured chocolate from a height to make it frothy.*

THE CACAO PLANTATIONS

When Cortés first set out on his voyage to the New World, his goal was to find El Dorado – Aztec gold. When he failed to unearth the dreamed-of riches, his attention turned to cacao beans. Having seen them used as currency, Cortés soon realized that money could literally be made to grow on trees. He devoted the next few years to exploiting the commercial potential of this "liquid gold" by setting up cacao plantations all around the Caribbean.

Before long, the Spanish had established plantations in Mexico, Ecuador, Venezuela, Peru, and the islands of Jamaica and Hispaniola (now called Haiti and the Dominican Republic). Cacao production has since spread all over the world, but the plantations in these original regions still produce the most highly prized varieties of bean.

THE SPANISH SECRET

The Spanish colonists tried to keep the secret of cacao production to themselves, for good reason – they were making fat profits out of processing the beans in Latin America before shipping them to Europe. However, the colonists did not keep their secret forever. In 1580, the first chocolate-processing plant was set up in Spain. From then on the popularity of chocolate spread to other European countries, which, in turn, established their own plantations, trade routes and processing facilities.

The Midas touch

Chocolate has always been associated with gold, possibly originating from Montezuma's ritual of drinking chocolate from a golden goblet, which, immediately after use, was thrown into the lake beside his palace. The lake turned out to be quite literally a gold mine for the Spanish after the conquest. Evidence of the association with gold can still be seen today with chocolate manufacturers, especially the Swiss, selling fake gold bars and chocolate coins encased in gold wrapping.

RIGHT:
Chocolate bars wrapped in foil to look like gold bars.

RITES, RITUALS AND CEREMONIES

The writings of New World travellers give us insights into the strange and sometimes barbaric rites, rituals and ceremonies attached to the cacao bean and the drinking of chocolate.

Religious rituals took place at different stages during cultivation. The Maya held a planting festival in honour of the gods during which they sacrificed a dog with a cacao-coloured spot in its fur. Another practice required planters to remain celibate for thirteen nights. They returned to their wives on the fourteenth night, and then the beans were sown.

FROM BEAN TO BEVERAGE

The Aztec drink bore little resemblance to the deliciously smooth, rich and creamy beverage we know today; it was bitter, greasy and served cold. Early travellers give differing accounts of how it was made. It seems that the grinding stone, or *metate,* was an important part of the production process. One writer describes the process in some detail: "For this purpose they have a broad, smooth stone, well polished and glazed very hard, and being made fit in all respects for their use, they grind the cacaos thereon very small". Because of the crude manual processing, the resulting liquor was full of shell, husks and pith.

A FROTHY BREW

The Jesuit José de Acosta wrote: "The chief use of this cacao is in a drink which they call chocolaté, whereof they make great account, foolishly and without reason: for it is loathsome to such as are not acquainted with it, having a skum or froth that is very unpleasant to taste, if they be not well conceited thereof."

For the Maya and Aztecs the froth was the most delicious part of the drink. The Maya made the drink frothy by pouring it from one bowl

BELOW: *A modern chocolate pot, whisk and chocolate from Colombia. The design of the whisk has not changed since the days of the Aztecs.*

to another from a height. Later, the Aztecs invented a device that the Spanish called a *molinillo* – a wooden swizzle stick with specially shaped paddles at one end, which fitted into the hole in the lid of the chocolate pot. The *molinillo* is still in use today.

The Spanish historian, Sahagún, describing a menu of chocolate drinks to be served to lords, tells us that there were "ruddy cacao; brilliant red cacao; orange cacao; black cacao; and white cacao". The likely flavourings for the lords' impressive choice of

Champurrado (chocolate atole)

The addition of maize would have turned the Aztec drink into a thin gruel or porridge known as atole. This is a type of fortified drink, not necessarily flavoured with chocolate, still served at meals or used as a pick-me-up by workers in the fields in Latin America today. The chocolate-flavoured version is always referred to as champurrado, from champurrar, meaning to mix one drink with another:

Put 65g/2^1/$_2$oz/^{1}/$_2$ cup masa harina (treated maize flour) or finely ground tortillas in a large pan with 750ml/1^1/$_4$ pints/3 cups water. Stir over low heat until thickened. Remove from the heat and stir in 175g/6oz/1 cup soft light brown sugar (or to taste), and 750ml/1^1/$_4$ pints/3 cups milk. Grate three 25g/1oz squares unsweetened chocolate and add to the pan. Beat well with a *molinillo* and serve steaming hot.

cacao were chilli, allspice, cloves, vanilla, a type of black pepper, various flower petals, nuts and annatto.

Sugar was not added until much later. There is a story that the nuns of Oaxaca, an Aztec town occupied by the Spanish until 1522, developed new recipes in deference to the Spanish sweet tooth. They added sugar and sweet spices, and so the bitter beverage of the Aztecs began its transformation to the delicious drink that we know today.

THE SPANISH VERSION

In 1701 an Englishman travelling in Spain gave a detailed and lengthy account of the manufacturing process developed by the Spanish. After the preliminary roasting, dehusking and grinding, the cocoa mass was ground again to a fine paste with plenty of sugar, cinnamon, vanilla, musk and annatto. The chocolate was formed into blocks, along the lines of modern block chocolate, but even so, these were still used only for making the beverage, rather than as confectionery.

As far as we know, this is the recipe that was used throughout Spain and the rest of Europe until the process was revolutionized in the 19th century by the technological achievements of the Dutchman Van Houten.

RIGHT: *Modern cocoa packaging based on the art nouveau style.*

VAN HOUTEN'S PRESS

In its early days chocolate was an extremely rich beverage. It contained a fatty substance, cocoa butter, which tended to rise to the top, where it would float in unappetizing greasy pools. Manufacturers overcame this to some extent by adding starchy substances to absorb the fat – a process similar to the Aztec tradition of adding ground maize.

Manufacturers had also tried unsuccessfully for years to devise a way of separating out the greasy cocoa butter. Breakthrough came in 1828 when, after years of trial and error, a Dutch chemist named Coenraad Van Houten patented a new and extremely efficient hydraulic press. His machine was able to extract about fifty per cent of the cocoa butter, leaving behind a refined, brittle, cake-like residue that could then be pulverized to a fine powder.

Not satisfied, Van Houten went one step further. He treated the powder with alkaline salts to improve the ease with which it could be mixed with water. Van Houten's inexhaustible patience completely revolutionized the chocolate industry. It led to the manufacture of what we now know as cocoa powder, which

in Van Houten's time was called "cocoa essence". It also led to an all-round improvement within the industry. Van Houten sold his rights ten years after he took out the patent, and the machine came into general use. Among the first customers were the Frys and the Cadburys, ever eager to outdo each other. Both firms were quick to enter the cocoa essence market, promoting the product's purity and ease of preparation. The old-style starch-based products were classified as adulterated, resulting in fierce legal battles between rival firms. Van Houten's press also initiated the industry's next step in gearing up – the large-scale production of chocolate as confectionery.

ABOVE: *An advertisement for Van Houten's cocoa powder – "the best liquid drinking chocolate".*

EATING CHOCOLATE

Having separated out the butter from the bean, the industry was left with the question of what to do with it – it was certainly too good to waste. One of the cocoa manufacturers – there are conflicting claims as to who was the first – hit upon the idea of melting the cocoa butter and combining it with a blend of ground cacao beans and sugar. The resulting mixture was a smooth and malleable paste that tolerated the added sugar without becoming gritty; the fat helped to dissolve it. The paste was thin enough to be poured into a mould and cast, and it is from this process that "eating chocolate" was developed.

The Fry family claim to have been the first to market the new product. Reflecting the current popularity of French-style products, they named the bars "Chocolat Délicieux à Manger" and exhibited them at a trade fair in Birmingham in 1849. The bars were a success, and eating chocolate caught on in a big way. Not to be outdone, Cadburys introduced the first box of small individual chocolates, followed by a Valentine's Day presentation box. Other companies, such as Bovril, began producing eating chocolate, and the new confectionery was established.

As a result of the new craze the price of cocoa butter rocketed and eating chocolate became an expensive sought-after product popular with society's élite. Meanwhile, cocoa was relegated to the masses.

The United States developed their version of chocolate bars a little later on. After experimenting with cream and chocolate – time and time again, the mixture scorched or failed to set – Milton Hershey's milk chocolate bars finally appeared on the market in 1900. His world-famous Kisses followed in 1907. Over on the west coast, Ghirardelli was making use of new chocolate-moulding technology, and soon added chocolate bars to their lines too. Specialist chocolate stores began to spring up all over the country and most towns had at least one well-respected establishment producing hand-made chocolates. The early chocolatiers were too small to import cacao beans or invest in expensive processing machinery. Instead, they bought industrial-sized blocks of coating chocolate from large companies such as Guittard and melted them down to use as "couverture" for their own hand-dipped fillings. Alice Bradley's 1917 Candy Cook Book, published in the United States, devoted a whole chapter to "Assorted Chocolates" with over sixty recipes for

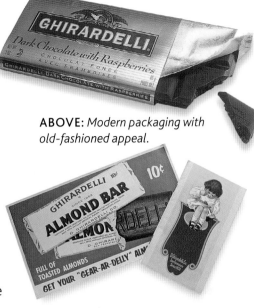

ABOVE: *Modern packaging with old-fashioned appeal.*

ABOVE: *Ghirardelli's first chocolate bars were "full of toasted almonds".*

fillings. Bradley stated: "More than one hundred different chocolates may be found in the price lists of some manufacturers."

The American chocolate industry got its biggest boost during the Second World War, when millions of chocolate bars were issued to the American armed forces in Europe. By this time both Ghirardelli and Hershey were well-equipped for the challenge of supplying them.

RIGHT: *Hershey's famous little Kisses were introduced in 1907.*

Growing chocolate

There are many stages in the processing of chocolate, and there has been a corresponding amount of development in its history as it has grown from a cold drink to the complex and adaptable substance it is today. This section traces the most important steps in the production of chocolate.

GROWING

The cacao bean grows in large pods on the cacao tree, *Theobroma cacao*, an evergreen that thrives in tropical areas lying between 20° north and 20° south of the equator. The tree is an exacting specimen, for it refuses to grow where it is too high, too cold or too dry, and it demands shelter from wind and sun. It also needs protection from wild animals, which delight in picking its pods, and it easily succumbs to various rots, wilts and fungal diseases.

It is traditional for the cacao tree to be grown under the protection of taller shade-creating trees, the conditions resembling its natural jungle habitat. In areas such as Grenada and parts of Jamaica, cacao trees grow successfully without additional shade, with sufficient moisture and nutrients in the soil. The cacao tree grows to about the size of an apple tree and starts bearing fruit in its third year. With luck, it will

continue to do so until at least its twentieth year, and it is not unknown for a tree to live to be one hundred years old. The glossy, dark green leaves, similar to those of the laurel, grow to nearly 30cm/12in long. The small, pale pink flowers grow in dense clusters straight out of the trunk and main branches on little raised cushions, a feature technically known as "cauliflory".

After pollination, flowers take about five months to develop into cacao pods. It's a colourful crop – the pods can be bright red, green, purple or yellow, changing hue as they ripen. Ripe pods are about 20cm/8in long, oval and pointed, each with 20 to 40 beans, embedded in a soft white pulp.

HARVESTING

It is by assessing the colour of the pod, and the sound it makes when tapped, that the picker can be sure

LEFT: *The cacao pods grow directly from the tree branches and change colour as they ripen.*

it is ready for picking. To be absolutely certain that the pod is ripe requires years of practice, and experienced pickers are highly valued.

The pods are removed from the tree by cutting through their stalks, those within reach with a cutlass, and those on higher branches with a curved knife fixed to a long pole. Cutting must be done with extreme care so as not to damage the "cauliflory", as this continually produces the flowers and therefore the fruit.

In some countries, harvesting takes place all year round, although most heavily from May to December. In other parts of the world, West Africa for instance, the main crop is harvested from September right through to February.

FERMENTING

The next stage is to split the pods with a cutlass, taking care not to damage the precious beans. These are scooped out, together with

Terms

Cacao is essentially the botanical name and refers to the tree, the pods and, at one time, the unfermented beans from the pods. The term is now also used for beans that have been fermented. Cocoa refers to the manufactured powder sold for drinking or food manufacturing purposes.

their surrounding pulp, and formed into a conical heap on a carefully arranged mat of banana leaves. When the heap is complete the leaves are folded over, and yet more of these giant leaves are added to enclose the heap completely. This is the start of the fermentation process, which lasts for up to six days.

The chemical processes involved in fermentation are complicated, but, basically, bacteria and yeasts present in the air multiply on the sugary pulp surrounding the beans, causing it to decompose to an acidic juice.

The process raises the temperature of the heap and under these conditions magical changes take place within the bean itself. The colour changes from purple to chocolate brown and the familiar cacao smell begins to emerge – the first crucial stage in developing

beans of superior quality. However, the fermentation process is sometimes omitted, with planters and manufacturers arguing both for and against.

DRYING

After fermentation, the beans are spread out on bamboo mats or wooden drying floors. During the ten to twenty days needed for drying, the beans are regularly turned to keep them well aired and to prevent moulds forming. In some places, where rainfall and humidity are very high, the beans are dried in commercial drying plants. However, the best quality cacao comes from beans that have been dried naturally in the warm tropical sun.

BELOW: *The precious cacao beans are separated from the pods before the fermentation process begins.*

Types of cacao bean

There are two distinct species of cacao bean used in the manufacture of chocolate: the criollo (meaning "native") and the forastero (meaning "foreign"). The criollo, the Rolls Royce of beans and the most delicate, is in a way a "limited edition", representing only 10 to 15 per cent of the world's production. It is cultivated mainly in the countries where cacao originated, namely Nicaragua, Guatemala, Mexico, Venezuela and Colombia, as well as Trinidad, Jamaica and Grenada. The criollo's exceptional flavour and aroma are prized by chocolate manufacturers the world over. Not surprisingly, the bean is always used in combination with other varieties.

The much hardier and higher-yielding forastero bean is grown mainly in Brazil and Africa, and it accounts for about 80 per cent of the world's production. It has a stronger, more bitter flavour than the criollo and is mainly used for blending. The one exception is the amenolado variety, known as the "Arriba" bean, grown in Ecuador. Its delicate flavour and fine aroma are considered equal to the world's best beans. Finally, there are also several hybrid beans, of which the trinitario is the best known. As the name suggests, it began life in Trinidad where, following a hurricane in 1727 that all but destroyed the plantations, it was a result of cross-breeding. It has both the robustness of the forastero and the delicate flavour of the criollo, and is used mainly for blending.

Modern manufacturing

Cacao beans arrive at a chocolate factory in the condition in which they leave the plantations. They have been fermented and dried but are still a raw material with the edible part enclosed inside the hard skin, which is dusty with the remains of the dried pulp.

ABOVE: *The beans are roasted to dehydrate them before grinding.*

ABOVE: *A chocolate manufacturer inspects a shipment of beans.*

CLEANING AND GRADING

The beans are given a preliminary cleaning, during which any stones or other objects are removed by sieving. The beans pass on a moving belt to storage hoppers, and from there they travel on another conveyor belt to the cleaning and grading machines where the beans are inspected. Any shrivelled or double beans are discarded, as is any undesirable material still clinging to the beans. Next, the beans are passed to the roasting machines.

ROASTING FOR FLAVOUR

This is a crucial part of the process and serves several functions. It develops the flavour and aroma, and it enriches the colour. Roasting also dries the husk surrounding the "nib", or edible inner part of the bean, making its removal easier.

The degree of roasting is very important. Overdoing it destroys the natural flavour of the bean, while under-roasting makes the

removal of the husk difficult. After roasting, the beans are cooled as quickly as possible to prevent further internal roasting.

WINNOWING

During the next stage, the beans are passed through the husking and winnowing machine, which cracks open the roasted beans, and blows the lighter husks away from the heavier pieces of nib. Manufacturers send the husks off for recycling as garden mulch, or use them to make soft "shell" butter.

THE CRUCIAL BLEND

During the blending process, specified quantities of different varieties of cacao nibs are weighed and transferred to a blender before they are then fed into the grinding machines.

The blending of beans for cocoa powder is generally less exacting than for eating chocolate. There are subtle differences of flavour in

each type of bean, and the final flavour is obtained by blending two, three or more types of bean after roasting.

GRINDING

In the grinding mill, the nibs pass through a series of rollers, resulting in coarse particles that turn into a warm paste. Then follows a second grinding to bring the particles down to the required size. After grinding, the cacao mass or "liquor" flows out of the machine into shallow metal containers.

THE PARTING OF THE WAYS

At this stage, further treatment of the liquor depends on whether it is to be made into cocoa powder or eating chocolate. For cocoa powder, the next step is the extraction of a large proportion of the cocoa butter. Some cocoa is "dutched", which helps to make cocoa powder much easier to mix with water. This also improves the colour and lightens the flavour.

Manufacturing eating chocolate

Cacao beans used for manufacturing eating chocolate are processed in a different way from beans used in cocoa manufacture.

MIXING

First, a carefully selected blend of roasted and ground nibs, the edible centre of the bean, is mixed with pulverized sugar and enriched with cocoa butter. The mixture then goes to the mélangeur, a round machine with a horizontal rotating base on which run heavy rollers. The chocolate paste that is discharged resembles well-kneaded dough.

For milk chocolate, powdered milk or evaporated sweetened milk is added to the ingredients in the mixer.

BELOW: Prolonged conching transforms the chocolate paste into velvety smoothness, as different flavours are added.

REFINING

Next, the chocolate paste is ground between a series of five rollers, each succeeding roller rotating faster than the previous one. The paste enters the first pair of rollers as a thin film, which is then taken up by the next pair, through a carefully adjusted gap. By the time the paste emerges from the fifth roller it is wafer-thin. The finest quality chocolate then needs further treatment known as "conching".

CONCHING

The conching machine was invented in 1880 by the Swiss chocolatier, Rodolfe Lindt. The name comes from the French (conche, meaning "shell") and is derived from the shape of the machine, a shell-shaped container. The function of the machine is to agitate the liquid chocolate very gently over a period that may be as long as seven days. It is a vital process in which the flavour of the chocolate is developed

BELOW: Luscious slices of crystallized fruit are carefully enrobed with smooth, dark chocolate.

and mellowed. During the conching process, various flavours are added, such as vanilla, cloves and cinnamon.

TEMPERING

Once conching is complete, the chocolate is fed into tempering kettles, where it is stirred and cooled but still remains liquid. Chocolate to be made into bars is pumped into moulding machines, while chocolate to be used as coating is pumped into enrobing machines.

MOULDING

Liquid chocolate is moulded into hollowed-out shapes, such as Easter eggs, which are then sometimes filled with individual chocolates.

ENROBING

Enrobing is the process of coating confectionery centres. This process is used not only for top-quality chocolates, but also for mass-produced chocolate bars.

BELOW: Hollow Easter eggs, filled with small chocolates, are a classic example of chocolate moulding.

A world of chocolate

In the next few pages, we survey some of the world's highest quality chocolate products. This is not a comprehensive selection, and it includes some of the most familiar quality brands as well as the more exclusive. Some products, such as the Toblerone bars, are internationally popular and universally available, and others, such as the exquisite chocolates made by the small specialist companies in America, are known to a much smaller market, but their first-class products are available by mail order and their market will increase as our appreciation of chocolate becomes more discerning.

BELGIUM

Ballotins are one of the most famous Belgian chocolates. These are chocolate-covered pralines, invented by Jean Neuhaus who, in 1912, developed coating chocolate capable of containing liquid fillings. Today Neuhaus is particularly well known for its flavoured Côte d'Or bars.

Of all Belgian chocolate companies, Godiva must be the most recognized. Established in 1929 by the Drap family, the company has 14-year-old Joseph Drap to thank for

ABOVE: *A selection of Kim's Cachet chocolates, exported worldwide.*

its success. Realizing people needed a little luxury in the austere post-war years, Joseph created the chocolate truffle. They were marketed under the name of Godiva and were a success.

Kim's, established in 1987 and manufacturer of the widely available luxury Cachet brand, specializes in handmade fillings. Kim's range includes white, milk and dark chocolate bars with luscious cream fillings such as hazelnut, coconut truffle, mocha and vanilla.

Pierre Colas specializes in unusual bars of chocolate flavoured with esoteric combinations of cardamom, juniper and lavender. The company supplies specialist retailers in Belgium, Spain, France and the London chocolate shop Rococo.

THE NETHERLANDS

Coenraad Van Houten, who revolutionized the chocolate industry with his cocoa press, was born in the Netherlands. With this background, it is not surprising that the Dutch chocolate industry today

concentrates largely on cocoa rather than eating chocolate. The four biggest companies, Van Houten, Bensdorp, De Zaan and Gerkens, were all set up in the nineteenth century and continue to supply the world with fine-quality cocoa powder.

GERMANY

The Germans are one of the largest consumers of chocolate in Europe. Faced with this demanding clientele, German chocolate manufacturers pride themselves on producing fresh, quality chocolates made with the very best ingredients.

Confiserie Heinemann, based in München-Gladbach and run by master chocolatier Heinz Heinemann, makes over sixty varieties of freshly made chocolates every day, including exceptional champagne truffles.

Feodora is probably Germany's best-known brand internationally. Their chocolate is wonderfully smooth due to lengthy conching.

AUSTRIA

Chocolate delicacies available in Austria include both pâtisserie and confectionery. A world-famous pâtisserie establishment is the Hotel Sacher, famous for its delectable Sachertorte, an apricot-glazed rich chocolate cake.

Altmann & Kühne, established in Vienna for more than eighty years, produce exquisite, hand-dipped miniature chocolates, in the most unusual shapes. The chocolates are beautifully packaged in miniature chests of drawers and treasure chests.

ITALY

Hazelnuts, chestnuts, almonds and honey have always been an integral part of Italian cuisine. It comes as no surprise, therefore, that Italians like their chocolate nutty and sweet. They also like their chocolate small, so bars are often sold in single serving sizes – handy for a quick fix, should the need arise. Neapolitans, which look exactly like miniature chocolate bars, complete with individual wrappers, are well-known throughout Europe.

The Italians are creative chocolate-makers, and they excel at presentation too; Italian packaging is stunning, whether the design is traditionally ornate or modern minimalist.

Caffarel in Turin is one of Italy's oldest chocolate-makers. Established in 1826, the company purchased a chocolate-making machine designed by Bozelli, a Genoese engineer, and so became the pioneers in setting out on the route to industrialization. In 1865 Caffarel developed Italy's favourite confection, *gianduja*, a rectangle of luscious chocolate and hazelnut paste, instantly recognizable by its triangular profile and rounded ends. Nowadays, most Italian chocolate-makers produce their own special version of *gianduja* using jealously guarded recipes. There is a glorious giant-sized version, *grangianduja*, as well as miniature *gianduiotti*.

Perugina, based in the medieval city of Perugia, Umbria, was set up in 1907 by Francesco Buitoni, a descendant of the well-known pasta-making family. From humble beginnings making sugared almonds,

ABOVE: *Gianduja chocolates are Italy's favourite confection.*

Perugina is now one of Italy's largest chocolate manufacturers. The most popular brand in their extensive range is *Baci* (kisses), introduced in 1922 and still going strong. Lovers still like to discover the romantic messages hidden under the wrapper.

SWITZERLAND

Three key developments have undoubtedly contributed to Switzerland's national preference for its very delicate, melt-in-the-mouth milk chocolate. Switzerland is the birthplace of Rodolphe Lindt, inventor of the conching machine that transforms chocolate from a rough gritty paste to a state of silky-smooth perfection. Lindt also created soft, creamy fondant chocolate by adding cocoa butter to the paste before conching. We have the Swiss to thank, too, for the invention of milk chocolate.

Sprüngli in Zurich is one of the world's most famous chocolate establishments. The shop in Bahnhofstrasse is renowned for its fresh *Truffes du Jour*, a heart-stopping mixture of finest chocolate, cream and butter, made to the highest standards. The company's worldwide delivery service guarantees a parcel's arrival within 24 hours of despatch.

Suchard in Berne is another long-established company, now owned by the American multinational Philip Morris. Suchard was a gold medallist several times over at the 1855 Exposition Universelle in Paris, and their milk chocolate bar, Milka, produced in 1901, is well known. Since 1970, Suchard have been the manufacturer of Toblerone bars, although these were originally produced by their inventor Jean Tobler. The bars were designed with a triangular profile representing the Swiss Alps. The name is derived from merging that of the inventor, Tobler, together with the word *torrone*, the Italian word for nougat. Toblerone is made with a blend of chocolate, nougat, almonds and egg white, and the bar is one of Switzerland's most popular products. Enthusiasts can enjoy giant bars, miniature bars and a whole range in between.

ABOVE: *The famous Toblerone bars.*

FRANCE

A large part of the French chocolate industry is made up of small, independent firms making ever more innovative *grand cru* chocolates to jealously guarded recipes. The French, who prefer dark, intensely flavoured chocolate, have a wide choice at their disposal.

Bernachon, a greatly respected family of artisan chocolatiers, set up in 1955 in Lyon. Sharing the caring attitude of the Quakers, the company provides daily lunch for the workers and, until recently, housed them in dormitories above the workshop. The Bernachons travel the world in search of the rarest cacao beans and the best nuts and fruit. Their chocolates are the very best. The range includes unusually flavoured chocolate bars, truffles, pralines and marzipans.

Bonnat in Voiron near Grenoble is one of the few companies that roasts its own beans. A purist at heart, master chocolatier Raymond Bonnat uses a single grand cru bean, rather than a blend, for each of the chocolates in his range. Bonnat's choice of seven crus, which consist of Côte d'Ivoire, Madagascar, Ceylon, Trinité, Chuao, Maragnan and Puerto

ABOVE: *One of Bonnat's superb grand cru bars.*

ABOVE: *A Chocolat Carpentier poster from 1895.*

Cabellois, is selected from the world's finest cacao plantations. Bonnat chocolates are available from specialist outlets in France, and from Mortimer and Bennett's shop in London, which is the sole British importer.

Cluizel, in Paris, is a family-run business set up in 1947, producing excellent chocolate with rare South American and African beans ground and roasted on the premises. It is perhaps best known for a small and very bitter chocolate bar containing 99 per cent cacao solids. Cluizel's chocolates are available throughout Europe.

The famous Fauchon shop in Paris was established in 1925 by Auguste Fauchon, whose passion was for collecting unusual merchandise. The company was taken over after his death by Joseph Pilosoff, whose granddaughter runs the business today. Fauchon specialities are the very best quality chocolate marrons glacés, truffles, pralines and ganaches, all exquisitely packaged.

La Maison du Chocolat in Paris was opened in 1977 by Robert Linxe, master chocolate-maker extraordinaire. Linxe's rigorous training and deep understanding of chocolate's complexities have played a major part in furthering the reputation of France's chocolate-makers. It was Linxe's collaboration with Valrhona which set the quality of their *grand cru* couvertures, which they, in turn, supply to smaller chocolate-makers. Linxe's specialities are exquisitely shaped squares, pyramids and lozenges of the very best dark and milk chocolate, filled with praline, buttery caramel or the lightest and creamiest ganache. The chocolates are sold in Paris and by leading specialist outlets in New York, Houston and Dallas.

Valrhona, set up in 1922 and based in the Rhône valley, is the leading supplier of couverture chocolate for smaller chocolate-makers. Its products include Carré, small chocolate squares made from individual bean varieties, packed in beautiful tins; BonBons de Chocolat, individual chocolates packed in gift boxes with a guide recommending the order in which they should be eaten; and the well-known Valrhona bars in their distinctive black wrappers. The cacao content of the bars ranges from 71 per cent for Noir Amer (bitter) to a high 40 per cent for Le Lacté (milk).

SPAIN

As recently as 1920, chocolate-makers in Spain were still using the curved granite *metate* for grinding cacao beans. The *chocolateros* would travel around with the *metate* strapped to their backs and bags of cacao beans under their arms. They would kneel on a little cushion in front of the stone and grind the beans in full public view so that buyers could be sure they were getting unadulterated stone-ground chocolate. Nowadays, chocolate-making in Spain is an industrialized process, but, even so, there are many small producers who still use traditional methods.

In some ways, Spanish chocolate is indistinguishable from quality chocolate made throughout Europe. But what sets it apart is the creativity and imagination of the chocolate-makers, and their use of the very best quality Mediterranean fruits and nuts.

Blanxart, set up in 1954 in Barcelona, is one of Spain's smaller specialist firms, producing handmade high-quality chocolates from the very best cacao beans. The mouthwatering range includes a delicate curl of candied Seville orange dipped in bitter chocolate, and clusters of chocolate-covered pine nuts, as well as liqueur-filled chocolates and praline.

Ludomar, in Barcelona, specializes in superior, made-to-order chocolates, which they sell to pâtisserie shops in Spain, France, Germany and Britain. Specialities are plump, chocolate-smothered cherries; *postre de músico*, a chocolate-covered cluster of fresh

almonds, hazelnuts and raisins; and *grageas*, almonds or hazelnuts drenched in chocolate or toffee.

Ramón Roca is a large company set up in Gerona in 1928 by the Roca family. Roca chocolates are said to be a favourite of former US Secretary of State Henry Kissinger, and they certainly grace the tables of Spain's society élite.

Valor in Villajoyosa, Alicante, was founded in 1881 by López Lloret, one of Spain's itinerant *chocolateros*. The fledgling enterprise has been handed down through three generations and is now one of Spain's largest and most technologically advanced chocolate companies, with a gleaming stainless-steel, fully computerized factory. Even though Valor has an enormous turnover and a vast range of products, the company prides itself on maintaining traditional quality, creativity and attention to detail.

Drinking chocolate is still widely enjoyed in Spain, and Valor is the country's leading producer. It is sold

ABOVE: *The Valor range of chocolates.*

both in powdered form and, more commonly, as a solid bar to be broken off as required and melted in foaming hot milk.

On the confectionery side, Valor's specialities are Chocolate Pearls – chocolate-covered almonds gathered from local almond groves; *doblones* – individually wrapped chocolate wafers; foil-wrapped hazelnut pralines and luxury chocolate bars filled with toffee, cream caramel or tiramisù.

ABOVE: *The Spanish love chocolate "a la taza" (in the cup).*

GREAT BRITAIN

During the last few years, British taste in chocolate has been undergoing a quiet revolution. Following the establishment of the Chocolate Society, a sort of sub-culture of chocolytes has emerged. Perhaps as a result of this new-found fervour, superior varieties of chocolate are increasingly finding their way into supermarkets, where they provide much-needed competition for the old-style sweet British milk chocolate.

Ackermans, a family firm founded in the mid-twentieth century by German-born Werner Ackerman and his wife, is one of the major producers of handmade chocolates in Britain. Ackermans has a shop in north London, and also supplies leading supermarkets and specialist outlets in Britain, mainland Europe and the United States. Its chocolates were a favourite with the late Queen Elizabeth the Queen Mother, who awarded the firm her Royal Warrant in 1969. Ackermans offers fresh cream truffles, chocolate-coated whole nuts, ginger wafers, hand-dipped crystallized fruits, and rose and violet fondant creams. It also produces a wonderful chocolate menagerie of hollow moulded hippos, crocodiles, bears and bunnies.

Bendicks of Mayfair, founded in the late 1920s by Colonel Benson

RIGHT: Organic chocolate made with beans grown by the Kechi Maya.

and Mr Dickson, was granted a Royal Warrant by Elizabeth II in 1962. Bendicks are famous for their excellent peppermint chocolates – an essentially British taste not shared by other European countries. Best-loved by connoisseurs are Bendicks Bittermints, a powerful mint fondant disc covered with smooth, dark unsweetened chocolate – a devastating combination. As well as the mint collection, Bendicks produces delicious truffles and chocolate-coated stem ginger.

Green and Black's, set up in the 1980s by Josephine Fairly, sells organic chocolate. The company launched with its Organic Dark Chocolate, followed by the "ethically correct" Maya Gold Organic Dark Chocolate, made with beans grown by the Kechi Maya in Belize, and flavoured with orange and spices. This product was the first in

ABOVE: *A selection of Ackermans chocolates, a favourite of British Royalty.*

Britain to be awarded the Fairtrade mark, which guarantees that small farmers are not exploited.

Rococo, in London's King's Road, is an Aladdin's cave of a shop founded in 1983 by chocolate enthusiast Chantal Coady. Using cacao from the world's finest plantations, Rococo specializes in *grand cru* single bean bars, artisan bars with exotic flavourings such as pink pepper and juniper, lavender, petitgrain and cardamom.

Terry's of York, founded in 1797, is perhaps alone among the mass-producers in manufacturing dark chocolate with a reasonable flavour. Their famous Chocolate Orange has been tucked in the toe of British children's Christmas stockings for generations, while their individually wrapped miniature Neapolitans have always been a welcome gift.

UNITED STATES

Chocolate consumers in the United States share the British liking for sweet milk chocolate, and the American chocolate industry is dominated by a small number of very large mass-producers who satisfy this national need. However, American taste has been changing. A number of small but sophisticated chocolate-makers have appeared on the scene and are taking advantage of the increasing popularity of European-style chocolate.

Dilettante, in Seattle, was established in 1976 by Dana Davenport, a third-generation chocolatier and descendant of Hungarian master chocolatier Julius Franzen. Their signature product is its Aristocrat range of chocolate truffles, flavoured with ginger, raspberries, hazelnuts, pecans or coffee. Dilettante also makes rich buttercream fondant, beautiful chocolate dragées with various coatings, and slim bars of chocolate.

BELOW: *Ghirardelli, new and old.*

Ghirardelli, founded in 1856 in San Francisco and one of America's pioneering chocolate-makers, produces quality eating chocolate, chocolate products for use in baking, and powdered drinking chocolate. Ghirardelli's Sweet Ground Chocolate with Cocoa has been a signature product for over a century. Although a mass-producer, Ghirardelli uses methods based on European traditions, producing bittersweet eating chocolate as well as the popular sweet milk varieties. Ghirardelli still grinds and roasts its own cacao beans shipped from quality plantations in Central and South America and West Africa. Its range includes milk, white and dark chocolate squares and attractively wrapped bars with tempting flavours such as raspberry, white mocha and biscotti, and double chocolate mocha.

Joseph Schmidt Confections was opened in San Francisco in 1983 by master chocolatier Joseph Schmidt and partner Audrey Ryan. Born in 1939 and raised in what was formerly known as Palestine, Schmidt looks to his Austrian roots for his skills. He was trained as a baker, but his supremely imaginative and sometimes outrageous creations show no

LEFT: *Joseph Schmidt's stunning and delicious truffles.*

evidence of this conventional background. Unusual in the chocolate world for his bold use of colour, and the large size of the individual chocolates, Schmidt's truffles gleam with perfect hand-painted spots of bright red or green, and his Slicks, thin chocolate discs, are beautifully painted in various colours. Special commissions include amazingly opulent sculpted creations for visiting dignitaries from abroad – including a giant panda for Prince Philip and a white dove for Nelson Mandela. Schmidt's chocolates are available from department stores in the United States and Harrods in London.

MEXICO

Chocolate as confectionery never really caught on in Mexico. The most important use of chocolate is still as a beverage, and as a flavouring in some of the special *moles* – rich, savoury sauces thickened with ground nuts and seeds. Chocolate is sold in rough, grainy tablets made with cacao, sugar, ground almonds and cinnamon – not so very different from the tablets made by the Spanish in the days of the conquistadors.

The most widely available brand outside Mexico is Ibarra, made by Chocolatera de Jalisco in Guadalajara, and packaged in a striking red and yellow striped hexagonal box. The tablets are delicious whipped to a froth in hot milk and served with *churros* (fried pastries).

Chocolate's therapeutic powers

The therapeutic properties of chocolate were much written about in the 17th and 18th centuries. The Aztec beliefs in the power of chocolate travelled with it, and great claims were made by manufacturers and converts alike for its powers as an antidote to exhaustion and weakness. Soldiers, scholars and clerics used it to keep them going during prolonged periods of physical, intellectual or spiritual endurance.

We now know that it is the fat and carbohydrate in chocolate which provide fuel for the body, and the fat content means that chocolate is digested slowly, thus maintaining a feeling of fullness and satiety. Even the iron content, which helps transport oxygen to the brain, may result in greater mental alertness, although this has yet to be proven.

NUTRITIONAL ANALYSIS

Although the relevance of nutritional analysis is questionable if the level of cacao solids or brand of chocolate used is not known, we can see from the comparative table, right, that dark chocolate, considered by the chocolate fraternity as infinitely superior, does not fare as well as might be expected.

Containing no milk, dark chocolate provides roughly half the protein of white and milk chocolate, and much less calcium. Protein is vital for the growth, repair and maintenance of the body; calcium is essential for muscle contraction, including the muscles which make the heart beat, and for healthy nerve function, enzyme activity and clotting of blood. Dark chocolate contains slightly less fat, something we are advised to cut down on, and comes out on top in terms of carbohydrate, magnesium (an essential constituent of our body cells and involved with releasing energy from the food we eat), iron (essential for the production of red blood cells, and for transporting oxygen around the body) and niacin (also involved in energy release from food). Dark chocolate also contains slightly fewer calories. White chocolate, sometimes dismissed by chocolate experts, contains more calcium, zinc, carotene and riboflavin (vitamin B2) than dark chocolate.

(per 100g)	Dark chocolate	Milk chocolate	White chocolate
Protein (g)	4.7	8.4	8.0
Fat (g)	29.2	30.3	30.9
Kilocalories	525	529	529
Carbohydrate (g)	64.8	59.4	58.3
Calcium (mg)	38	220	270
Magnesium (mg)	100	55	26
Iron (mg)	2.4	1.6	0.2
Zinc (mg)	0.2	0.2	0.9
Carotene (vitamin A) (mcg)	40	40	75
Vitamin E (mg)	0.85	0.74	1.14
Thiamin (vitamin B1) (mg)	0.07	0.10	0.08
Riboflavin (vitamin B2) (mg)	0.08	0.23	0.49
Niacin (vitamin B3) (mg)	0.4	0.2	0.2
Vitamin B6 (mg)	0.07	0.07	0.07
Vitamin B12 (mcg)	—	trace	trace
Folate (mcg)	10	10	10
Vitamin C	0	0	0

Source: McCance and Widdowson's *The Composition of Foods*, fifth edition.

RIGHT: *A platter of high-quality hand-made chocolates is every chocolate lover's fantasy.*

A NATURAL STIMULANT

As well as the more well-known nutrients, chocolate also contains certain alkaloids – organic substances found in plants – which have a potent effect on the body. The most important is theobromine, which stimulates the kidneys as a mild diuretic. Chocolate is also a stimulant of the central nervous system, producing an effect similar to caffeine, which is also present in chocolate. Theobromine makes up about two per cent of the cacao bean and about 200mg finds its way into an average-sized bar of chocolate. The caffeine content is much smaller – about 25mg per bar, which is roughly one quarter the amount found in a cup of coffee.

ABOVE: *19th-century advertising for homeopathic chocolate products.*

Myths and prejudices

Claims that chocolate is bad for you are almost certainly based on the excess sugar and added vegetable fat in poor grade, mass-produced chocolate. Quality chocolate contains pure cocoa butter with no other fat, as well as a high percentage of cacao solids and less sugar. Claims that chocolate causes migraine, obesity, acne, tooth decay and allergies have also been refuted by medical experts.

Migraine: Cheese and chocolate have been cited as the cause of migraine, which can be set off by large doses of tyramine. Chocolate, however, contains a very small quantity of tyramine, far less than cheese.

Obesity: Good-quality dark chocolate is unlikely to be the cause of obesity because it contains far less sugar than cheap chocolate and, because it is more expensive, is less likely to be eaten to excess.

Acne: American surveys show no correlation between chocolate consumption and acne. Likely culprits are hormonal imbalances and a lack of fruit and vegetables in the diet.

Tooth decay: Chocolate melts in the mouth and so is in contact with teeth for only a short time. While the sugar content will contribute to tooth decay, the risk is far less than that of sticky sweets, which are in the mouth longer.

Allergy: Less than two per cent of the population has a genuine food allergy, and chocolate allergies are rare. It is more likely to be the nuts and milk in chocolate that are the cause, so check the ingredients.

Chocolate and the mind

The question of whether or not chocolate is an addictive substance always raises spirited discussion. Some social historians have even reported tales of chocolate addiction and associated crimes committed in order to satisfy an ever-increasing need.

Some medical experts believe that the theobromine and caffeine in chocolate are the cause of its so-called addictive properties, but it may well be the presence of another substance called phenylethylamine. This is one of a group of chemicals known as endorphins, which have an effect similar to amphetamine, to which phenylethylamine is related. When released into the bloodstream, endorphins lift the mood, creating positive energy and feelings ranging from happiness to euphoria, as experienced in the runner's "high" or the aerobic exerciser's "burn". Phenylethylamine is also naturally present in the human body. Levels in the brain have even been found to increase when we experience the state we refer to as "falling in love", which is why we experience that feeling when we eat good chocolate.

CRAVING AND ADDICTION

Chocolate lovers would do well to be aware of the difference between craving and addiction.

ABOVE: *French doctors believed chocolate was beneficial for chronic illnesses.*

Craving is an unmet desire for a substance, whether it be chocolate, hot buttered toast, or a cup of coffee. The craving is usually brought on by stress, and the desired substance usually diffuses the stress more effectively than other means, and may actually, as a result, enhance a person's performance by increasing concentration and reducing fatigue.

Addiction, on the other hand, is defined as the habitual use of a substance, which becomes less and less effective at satisfying the need and results in unpleasant withdrawal symptoms should any attempt be made to give up the substance in question. Chocolate hardly comes into the addictive category, although it has been said that the glucose in chocolate triggers a release in the production of endorphins – the body's natural opiates – which in turn can lead to a cycle of craving.

WOMEN'S CRAVING AND CHOCOLATE

Women are the greatest consumers of chocolate, and several studies have sought to explain why.

Psychiatrists have suggested that the mechanism that regulates body levels of phenylethylamine may be faulty in some women. This may explain a tendency to binge on chocolate after an emotional upset – it is an instinctive form of self-medication to treat the imbalance of mood-controlling chemicals.

It must be said, however, that although statistically it may be the case that more women buy chocolate than men, it is also true that for both sexes, and for people of all ages, chocolate can be many things. There are probably many women who could instantly name men whose chocolate consumption is more regular and compulsive than theirs, and it is perhaps one of the many cultural myths that women are more addicted to it than men. What we can say is that the seduction of chocolate, and its comforting allure, is as strong in the present as it was for the Maya warrior princes and princesses of the 4th century.

BELOW: *A deeply indulgent and luxurious chocolate experience.*

Chocolate and love

Chocolate has long been associated with passion and its reputation as an aphrodisiac can be traced back to the days of the Aztecs and the Spanish conquistadors. Conclusions were obviously drawn from the Emperor Montezuma's liking for copious flagons of chocolate before retiring to his harem.

Historical sources abound with tales of chocolate being used as an aphrodisiac. Casanova is believed to have thought that hot chocolate was "the elixir of love", and drank it instead of champagne!

In the following tale, the Marquis de Sade uses both chocolate and the notorious aphrodisiac Spanish Fly to amuse his guests: "Into the dessert he slipped chocolate pastilles so good that a number of people devoured them ... but he had mixed in some Spanish fly ... those who ate the pastilles began to burn with unchaste ardour ... Even the most respectable of women were unable to resist the

LEFT: *Chocolate almonds make a perfect gift to a loved one.*

uterine rage that stirred within them. And so it was that M. de Sade enjoyed the favours of his sister-in-law."

THE GREAT INFLAMER

Brandon Head, in *The Food of the Gods*, reported that even after chocolate had become widely accepted as a nourishing beverage, it was still regarded by some "as a violent inflamer of passions, which should be prohibited to the monks".

In 1905 a journalist writing in the British *Spectator* magazine issued dire warnings: "I shall also advise my fair readers to be in a particular manner careful how they meddle with romances, chocolates, novels, and the like inflamers, which I look upon as very dangerous to be made use of..."

SENSUAL ASSOCIATIONS

Although contemporary scientific research suggests that chocolate does not contain substances of a directly aphrodisiac nature, modern advertising clearly links chocolate with sensuality. Chocolate is invariably depicted as a "naughty" indulgence, often appearing in scenes heavy with sexual innuendo.

Advertising also demonstrates a definite gender bias by targeting women as the primary users. Most

LEFT: *Advertising has always used chocolate's link with sensuality.*

advertisements show chocolate being enjoyed by beautiful women, or chocolates being offered to them by a man. The association between women, sensuality and chocolate was reinforced by the cinema, too. A common image in the 1930s was the glamorous *femme fatale*, languorously working her way through a lavish box of chocolates.

CHOCOLATE AND CHILDHOOD

The association with love and nurture was also exploited by manufacturers. The earliest cocoa tins portrayed nursemaids serving mugs of chocolate to children, and advertising made much of the wholesomeness of chocolate, with posters of healthy children enjoying cups of chocolate in the fresh air. The first chocolate boxes showed sentimental images of young girls, flowers and kittens.

Chocolate plays a large part in childhood the world over in the form of Christmas treats, Easter eggs, birthday presents, or bribes from parents coaxing their offspring to behave well. Encouraged as most of us are to be passionate about chocolate from an early age, it is no wonder we carry that ardour with us through childhood and beyond.

Flavourings and fillings

Every chocolate manufacturer has a secret condiment or blend of flavourings that he or she claims gives their product a unique character. Fillings and flavourings from the same tropical latitude as the cacao bean itself – vanilla, cinnamon, cardamom, coffee, rum, ginger, even pepper and chilli – are the ones most commonly used. Even in this age of "culinary fusion", when we happily mix and match cuisines in our never-ending quest for novelty, flavouring chocolate with spices from a more northerly latitude can simply seem odd – it is hard to imagine fennel or caraway-flavoured chocolate, for instance – but perhaps it is just a matter of time before it happens successfully.

ABOVE: *Handmade "tartufini" from southern Italy – whole almonds coated in praline and dusted with dark cocoa and powdered sugar.*

SECRET FLAVOURS

Every chocolate-consuming country has its favourite flavourings. Italy prefers its chocolate mixed with hazelnuts, almonds or chestnuts. France likes a nutty flavour too, but strongly flavoured dark bitter chocolate is also popular there. Spain likes spiced chocolate, and fillings such as almonds and dried fruits, America consumes mostly milk chocolate, often with whole peanuts or almonds

embedded in it, while Britain likes vanilla. Not only that, every country uses different blends of beans, and, as already mentioned, the subtle variations in the flavour of different bean varieties play their part in determining the final flavour of the chocolate. If we also take into account different processing methods used by individual factories, the number of flavour combinations is endless.

Within the scientific community, the complexity of chocolate's flavour is a source of enormous fascination to the flavour scientists who are regularly producing learned papers on the subject. Daniel Querici, speaking at the Oxford Symposium on Food and Cookery, summed up the subject of chocolate's flavour in a delightful way: "Its complex flavour profile looks like a royal peacock tail, although not fully deployed, as food scientists keep discovering new components."

Fillings

Boiled: based on sugar and glucose and including caramels, butterscotch and fudge.

Creams and fondants: a mixture of sugar crystals in a sugar syrup, with fruit or other flavourings, coated with tempered chocolate.

Croquet (or brittle): caramelized sugar with crushed nuts.

Ganache: a mixture of chocolate, cream and butter, either rolled in cocoa powder to make a truffle or enrobed in tempered chocolate.

Gianduja: finely ground nuts and sugar mixed with dark or milk chocolate.

Marzipan: sugar syrup mixed with ground almonds, coated with dark or milk chocolate.

Nougat: a mixture of beaten egg white, boiled sugar, nuts and/or candied fruit. Known as *Montélimar* in France, *torrone* in Italy, and *turrón* in Spain.

Praline: similar to *gianduja* but with a coarser texture and usually coated with dark or milk chocolate.

FANTASTIC FILLINGS

Chocolate has been used as a coating for anything from almonds and dried fruit to bizarre ingredients such as ants, and a look at the contents of a global box of chocolates will reveal many more.

In the United States, chillies and chocolate come together once more in the whacky confectionery range created by two chocolatiers from Oregon. Their products, which won an award at the Fiery Foods Show at Albuquerque, New Mexico, include Mexican Zingers, a creamy, green jalapeño salsa encased in a white chocolate shell, and Southwest Coyote Kickers, a red jalapeño salsa cream covered in light milk chocolate.

Although chilli-filled chocolates are legal in the United States, alcoholic fillings are not universally acceptable. As recently as 1986, only one American state permitted the manufacture of alcoholic chocolates, only eleven states permitted their sale, and, even then, the permitted alcohol levels were severely restricted.

In Europe, however, it is a different story. In Italy, smooth dark chocolates are filled with decadent liqueur-soaked fruits – cherries, kumquats, slices of dried peach, pear and apricot. There are also plump prunes, dates and walnuts filled with marzipan and covered with dark chocolate.

In Britain, chocolate lovers can enjoy delicate fondant fillings such as violet and rose creams or marzipan; truffle fillings laced with champagne, Cointreau or Drambuie; or chunks of stem ginger, and whole brazil nuts. France is the birthplace of the dusky chocolate truffle created in the late nineteenth century by the Duc de Praslin, one of Louis XIV's ministers. At that time it was considered amusing to create a food resembling something totally unrelated. *Truffes au chocolat* were deeply rich, buttery chocolate balls that were then rolled in dark cocoa powder to resemble the savoury black fungi from Périgord. The dragée is a French confectionery classic that, in its original form – almonds coated with sugar and honey – dates

back to the 13th century. The dragée adapted well to the introduction of chocolate and now consists of praline or nuts covered in chocolate and a hard sugar coating.

A filling story

In 1987, Ethel M Chocolates, owned by 82-year-old Forrest Mars and named after his mother, attempted to introduce liqueur-filled chocolates to Las Vegas, Nevada. The chocolates were spiked with crème de menthe, brandy, Scotch and bourbon. Mr Mars found that the sale and manufacture of alcoholic chocolates was illegal in most American states. Things were not looking good, especially as an appeal to legalize alcoholic chocolates had recently been rejected in Pennsylvania, home of Hersheyville.

As was to be expected, the squeaky-clean Hershey Company added their support to the rejection on the grounds that "liquor-laced chocolates are inconsistent with values emphasized by religious and medical communities".

Not one to give up easily, the determined Mr Mars successfully petitioned for the sale and manufacture of alcoholic chocolates in his home state of Nevada. This meant he could sell his chocolates there but not across the border, and so he had to content himself with selling to the twenty million tourists who visited Las Vegas each year. Ethel M Chocolates are still to be found at Las Vegas airport and in many of the city's luxury hotels.

ABOVE: *Handmade British chocolates with melt-in-the-mouth fondant fillings, delicately flavoured with violet and rose.*

ABOVE: *Italian chocolates from Maglio, with succulent fillings of walnuts, dried fruit and pistachio marzipan.*

Types of chocolate

There is a wealth of wonderful chocolate products available, with an often confusing array of types, qualities, fillings and flavourings. Here is a brief guide to what you should look for and how to enjoy chocolate at its best.

DARK (BITTERSWEET) AND PLAIN (SEMISWEET) CHOCOLATE

Dark chocolate must contain a minimum of 34 per cent cacao solids, but generally, the higher the proportion, the better. Dark chocolate containing just 30 per cent cacao solids used to be considered high quality. Now, as taste and awareness of chocolate grows, 60 per cent is the preferred minimum, while, for chocoholics, 70–80 per cent is more desirable.

High-quality dark chocolate contains a very small proportion of sugar. Adding sugar to chocolate has been compared with adding salt to food. You need just enough to enhance the flavour but not so much that it is destroyed. Quality chocolate contains pure vanilla, an expensive flavouring sometimes called Bourbon Vanilla, extracted from an orchid grown in Madagascar. It also contains the minutest amount of lecithin, a vegetable stabilizer. In unsweetened chocolate, found only in specialist shops, cacao solids are as high as 98 per cent.

ABOVE: *Couverture chocolate, which has a very high proportion of cacao solids.*

COUVERTURE

This is high-quality chocolate in the professional league, used mainly for coating and in baking. Couverture usually has a minimum of 32 per cent cocoa butter, which enables it to form a much thinner shell than ordinary chocolate.

MILK CHOCOLATE

To some aficionados, milk chocolate is not really chocolate, but, increasingly, there are good brands around, although they may be

BELOW: *Best quality couverture with a good sheen. Blocks like this are supplied to chocolatiers.*

difficult to find. A good brand will have a cacao solid content of around 40 per cent, but most mass-produced milk chocolate contains only 20 per cent.

Mass-produced milk chocolate has a very high sugar content, up to 65 per cent. It can also contain up to 5 per cent vegetable fat, which is used as a substitute for expensive cocoa butter, and artificial flavouring.

Formula for quality chocolate

56–70% cacao solids, to include 31% cocoa butter
29–43% finely ground sugar
1% lecithin and pure vanilla extract

Formula for mass-produced milk chocolate

11% cacao solids
3% vegetable fat
20% milk solids
65% sugar
1% lecithin and synthetic vanillin

WHITE CHOCOLATE

This is basically cocoa butter without any cacao solids, with some added sugar, flavouring and milk. White chocolate does not have the same depth of flavour as dark chocolate. It is mainly sold for its novelty value or to provide an attractive colour contrast in chocolates and chocolate desserts. The best quality brands tend to be French and Swiss. British brands usually contain vegetable oil instead of cocoa butter, as well as synthetic flavourings.

ASSESSING QUALITY

All our senses – sight, smell, sound, touch and taste – come into play when assessing the quality of dark chocolate. There are several points to watch out for.

Appearance: The chocolate should be smooth, brilliantly shiny and pure mahogany-black in colour.

Smell: The chocolate should not smell excessively sweet.

Sound: The chocolate should be crisp and make a distinct "snap" when broken in two. If the chocolate splinters, it is too dry; if it resists breaking, it is too waxy.

Touch: Chocolate with a high cocoa butter content should quickly start to melt when held in the hand – this is a good sign. In the mouth, it should feel ultra-smooth with no hint of graininess, and it should melt instantly.

RIGHT: A bloom has formed on the surface of the chocolate on the right. An unaffected piece on the left shows the difference in appearance.

Taste: Chocolate contains a kaleidoscope of flavours and aromas which continue to develop in the mouth. The basic flavours are bitterness with a hint of acidity, sweetness with a suggestion of sourness, and just a touch of saltiness, which helps release the aromas of cocoa, pineapple, banana, vanilla and cinnamon.

STORAGE

Humidity and heat are chocolate's greatest enemies; both can cause a "bloom" to appear on the surface. Heat-induced bloom is the result of cocoa butter crystals rising to the surface and recrystallizing. The flavour is unaffected but the appearance is spoiled.

Humidity-induced bloom is more damaging. It is a result of sugar crystals being drawn to the surface, where they dissolve in the moist atmosphere and eventually recrystallize to form an unpleasant grey coating. As the texture and taste of the chocolate deteriorate, too, chocolate that has suffered in this way should be thrown away. The ideal temperature for storing chocolate is 10–15°C (50–60°F), slightly warmer than the refrigerator, and the humidity

Tasting techniques

If your chocolate is correctly stored, you will need to allow an hour or so for it to reach the recommended temperature of 19–25°C/66–77°F.

Dark chocolate: Allow the chocolate to sit in your mouth for a few moments to release its primary flavours and aromas. Then chew it five to ten times to release the secondary aromas. Let it rest lightly against the roof of your mouth so that you experience the full range of flavours. Finally, enjoy the lingering tastes in your mouth.

Filled chocolate: Allow the chocolate to sit in your mouth for a few moments to release its primary flavours and aromas. Then chew it three to five times to mix the chocolate and the filling. Let the mixture melt slowly in your mouth so that you experience a new range of flavours. Enjoy the lingering tastes.

should be 60–70 per cent. Chocolate also absorbs surrounding odours extremely easily and so it should always be kept in an airtight container in a cool place.

Index